HOW
NOT
TO BE
STUPID

HOW NOT TO BE STUPID

IGOR SIBALDI

Translated from the Italian by Emily Boyce

PAN BOOKS

First published in the UK 2026 by Pan Books
an imprint of Pan Macmillan
The Smithson, 6 Briset Street, London ECIM 5NR
EU representative: Macmillan Publishers Ireland Ltd, 1st Floor,
The Liffey Trust Centre, 117–126 Sheriff Street Upper,
Dublin 1 D01 YC43
Associated companies throughout the world

ISBN 978-1-0350-9497-4

Originally published 2025 in Italy as *Come non essere stupidi* by Mondadori Libri S.p.A., Milano

1 3 5 7 9 8 6 4 2

A CIP catalogue record for this book is available from the British Library.

Typeset in Janson Text LT Std by Six Red Marbles UK, Thetford, Norfolk
Printed and bound in the UK using 100% Renewable Electricity by CPI Group (UK) Ltd

Visit **www.panmacmillan.com** to read more about
all our books and to buy them.

CONTENTS

Part One: Practical

Epilogue:
Analysing Ourselves and Others

PART ONE

Practical

WHAT IS STUPIDITY?

The word 'stupid' enters our personal vocabulary in our earliest years. By the age of four, we already know how it feels to be called stupid, in the three harshest inflections of the term:

'Stupid!'

'You're stupid.'

'You're a stupid boy/girl.'

'Stupid!' is a warning shot. It means: look out, you're about to step over a psychological line nobody wants to cross, and there's no easy way back.

'You're stupid' is a diagnosis. It means: you've gone over that line and now you're in trouble. Call for help and cross your fingers it doesn't get any worse.

'You're a stupid boy/girl' is an indictment. It means: there are stupid people in the world, a woefully obtuse bunch who cause nothing but harm, and you're one of them.

We also learn early on to say it of other people: 'He's a stupid boy.'

Uttering these words makes us feel better, because the

implication is, 'If I've noticed he's stupid, there's a good chance I'm not.'

Since childhood, the relief at avoiding stupidity, the fear of crossing the line into stupidity, or the shame of having done so, have been so strong they have made us believe we know what stupidity is. Especially since, when we have used the word, nobody has ever asked, 'OK, but stupid in what way?' And we have never asked, either, for fear of looking stupid.

Supposing we asked ourselves the question now, we would struggle to find an answer. Describing exactly what we mean by the word 'stupidity' is as difficult as explaining what a strawberry tastes like. Saying, 'Well, being stupid means not being intelligent,' is like saying that strawberries don't taste like cherries. What, then, if not cherries? If stupid people are not intelligent, then what are they?

The difficulty in both cases is the same, but for different reasons. In the case of strawberries, there's a linguistic gap: we don't have the right vocabulary to describe the delicious flavour we all know. Stupidity, on the other hand, would be perfectly describable if, as we'll discover in the next chapter, we were not held back by a kind of social block: 'stupid' is a *conventional word* – just like 'reality', 'politics' and so on. And conventional words are like the rules of a game: they are accepted at face value and never questioned, simply because everyone uses them. Just as there's no need to understand why, in a game of chess, the bishop only moves diagonally (and it would be pointless asking), calling someone stupid or being afraid to be seen as stupid doesn't require you to know exactly what stupidity is, and so the question goes unasked.

The game in which we use conventional words like 'reality', 'politics' and 'stupid', among many others, is called 'fitting in'. It begins at birth, and it never ends. It's not especially challenging, it's not fun, and those who take part in it consider it not a game but an essential part of everyday life. Some say it does more harm than good; others call it conformism.

Another more challenging and even less fun game is war, and this, too, is full of conventional words ('enemy', 'general', 'order', 'soldier', 'civilian', etc.) which must under no circumstances be questioned for as long as the game is in play. In fact, were they to be called into question *during the war*, the whole thing would come to a halt, and the players would be left looking like idiots.

It almost always works this way with conventional words: they allow you to talk about the things you're supposed to talk about, without thinking.

And, above all, this book aims to argue against conventional words.

QUESTION: 'So "reality" is a conventional word?'

ANSWER: 'Yes. We'll go over this again later.'

WHAT STUPIDITY IS

Stupidity, then, is derived from the Latin *stupeo*, meaning 'I remain still'. A stupid person (*stupidus*) may seem to be ignorant, foolish, imbecilic, silly, crack-brained, cretinous, idiotic or weak-minded, might be branded an ass, asshole or dickhead, but isn't necessarily any of these things: a stupid person is just someone who has to stand still sometimes, because they don't know how to react to situations which appear straightforward to others.

Let's study this a little more closely.

An *ignoramus*, in Latin, 'doesn't know', and a stupid person may be very ignorant, but not everyone who is ignorant is stupid: some are resourceful, successful and self-assured, because their ignorance shields them from doubt, and they look down on or pity the *stupidus*.

A feature of many a Shakespearean comedy, the *fool* (from the Latin *follis*, 'bellows') is a windbag, an empty, inflated thing. Fools lack intelligence but may not know it, or rather it's very likely they don't know it, in which case, like the ignoramus, they can go far, considering themselves equipped to handle every situation life throws at them – unlike the *stupidus*.

Imbeciles can't manage on their own: they don't have a *becillum*, a staff or support in Latin, to prop them up. But all is not lost: they just need to find someone or something to lean on – a family, a partner, a faith, an ideal, a series of stereotypes – and they can overcome all their problems. The *stupidus* won't find these things, nor even look for them.

Silly people are inane, blandly trivial, careless, easily led. They have always been in the majority. As a cardinal conveniently said five centuries ago, *Vulgus vult decipi*, 'people want to be deceived'. His words still ring true today. Indeed, for the past few decades, silly people have been coddled by many – our media-speak, belief systems and recipes for happiness are tailored to their measure. Silly people are, more than ever, the norm; the *stupidus* is not.

Those who are *crack-brained* or crackpots have allowed themselves to be broken by a bad experience. Or, they're silly people with a life story that might interest a psychologist. What I said about silly people also applies to them.

Cretin is a Gallicism, from *crétin*, meaning defective, deranged, born mentally deficient (words which, like moron, retard and imbecile, were once used by scientists to describe intellectual disabilities). It's a cruel barb for someone who is irredeemably obtuse; I've never encountered anyone deserving of the term.

Idiots (from the ancient Greek *ídios*, 'particular', 'exclusive') spend too much time alone and tend to think in a way that makes sense only to themselves. An idiot is rarely a *stupidus*: the *stupidus* doesn't like to be alone and, most importantly, doesn't think much.

Weak-minded, spineless or wimpish people only run into

problems when they don't confine themselves to mixing with others of the same ilk. The *stupidus* doesn't feel at home among wimps, nor even among other stupid people.

An *ass* is a donkey, but in North American English, also a person's rear end, and *assholes* (or arseholes) are sly, ill-intentioned and two-faced, masters at profiting from others' faults or weaknesses: the scatological term used to mark them out is a warning to keep your distance. The *stupidus* is not sly: if a *stupidus* takes advantage of someone, it's usually by accident.

A *dickhead* (or *knob*, *bell end* or *tool*, or any number of other terms related to the male member) is fickle and unreliable, associated with masculine excitability and a tendency for the haphazard, often barking up entirely the wrong tree. The *stupidus* is timid, and not plucky enough to go barking up.

The *stupidus* has another unique characteristic besides those alluded to above: he or she is never completely stupid. No one stays permanently still, incapable of reacting in any given circumstance. You can be stupid in some areas and not in others. Stupid people can also be very intelligent, from time to time.

And they know it.

QUESTION: 'Does knowing it make them sad?'

ANSWER: 'Usually, yes.'

STUPID IN WHAT WAY?

There are twelve areas of experience in which we can be stupid – at least, that's as many as I've counted. They are:

Let's call them functions. All of us have all of them, and they each play a part in shaping the world as we see it.

We learn, act, think, desire, remember and forget through these functions, in the following ways:

Communication is letting others (and ourselves) know that we exist, and what exists for us;

Self-Defence is being, or not being, scared;

External Direction is knowing where we're going and where we are;

Internal Direction is knowing how we know what we know, and how to find out more;

Authority is our own, and that of others;

Wealth is what we can afford, or what we afford or allow ourselves;

Our relationship with *The Past* is what interests us about the generations that have gone before us;

Your Past is what matters to us about our own lived experience;

The *Outsider* function is our capacity to differentiate ourselves from others;

Our *Sense of Obstacles* is knowing what's stopping us and why;

Overcoming Obstacles is knowing how and why to move forward;

Attention is noticing what the other functions are
causing or not causing to happen.

Over the next few chapters, I'll explain how to analyse
these twelve functions, which produce our realities and
unrealities. They are as powerful as they are fragile, and can
easily be impeded, becoming stuck or stupefied. Thankfully,
the sticking points can be remedied, as long as you notice
them. What I referred to earlier as the game of fitting in,
with its lexicon of conventional words, affects each and
every one of these functions: we'll see how, in a series of
digressions. A comprehensive picture will emerge of the *way*
in which we create, and of *what* we create every day (which
is usually too little).

QUESTION: 'Why have you laid out these functions in a
circle?'

ANSWER: 'Because they provide us with a kind of
compass, and for a couple of other theoretical reasons
I'll go into in the second part of the book.'

QUESTION: 'Are you saying we're all inside the circle?'

ANSWER: 'Yes.'

COMMUNICATION

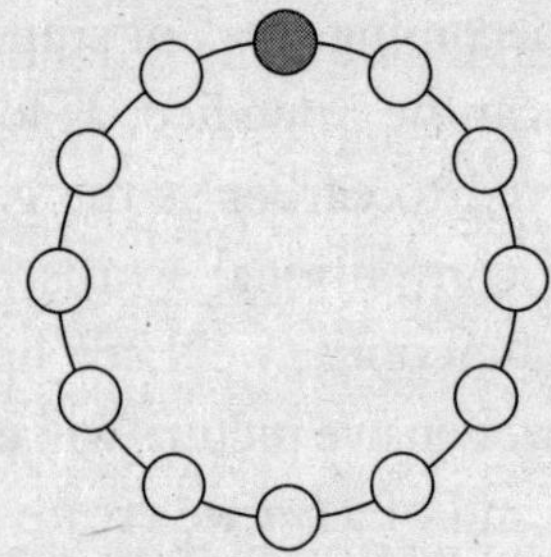

Do I express what I feel?

We all know what communication is, and how important it is. What's less well known, but a matter of great import-ance, is what impedes (or stupefies) communication on a daily basis.

If I didn't know the word 'gladiolus', I wouldn't know I was looking at a gladiolus when I saw one. That's not to say gladioli wouldn't exist for me; I would still see them, and could still buy them from a florist: 'I'll have half a dozen of those flowers, please.' There are many things which exist even if we don't know what they're called, but we can't talk about things whose names we don't know unless they're right in front of us.

So the fewer words we know, the less we can describe,

imagine, desire. The fewer words we know, the more we
find ourselves confined to 'the here and now'.

> THE HERE AND NOW: a situation and expression
> once beloved of right-wing thinkers (closely
> linked to the fascist *squadristi* motto '*Me ne
> frego*' – 'sod it', implying 'I don't give a damn
> about the past, and I don't give a damn about
> the consequences'). These days, devotees
> of cod spirituality, and some psychologists,
> are equally fond of focusing on the present.
> 'The here and now' is, by nature, the spatial-
> temporal dimension of those who have nothing
> to look forward to in the future and who place
> no importance on the past, nor, therefore, on
> friendship, love or other human bonds built up
> slowly over time. Inevitably, those who confine
> themselves to the here and now are at the mercy
> of those with broader horizons.

Limited to the few words available in the here and now,
communication is sparse, and the mind burdened by things
left unresolved, unconfessed to others or ourselves. We can
only move on from a mistake if we can explain exactly how
and why we were mistaken; we can only make use of a talent
to the extent that we can express – to ourselves, first of all,
and then to others – what that talent consists of. Otherwise
we're stuck, and that's stupidity.

Wretched, therefore, is the life of those with scant active vocabulary.

> ACTIVE VOCABULARY: the number of words
> a person is readily able to use. For example,
> 'table' and 'chair' are part of everybody's
> active vocabulary; 'existential', on the other
> hand, figures in the active vocabulary of
> relatively few.

Our active vocabulary is an existential factor, in the sense that it shapes our very existence: it defines the spatial-temporal scope of the world in which we can find, or indeed lose, our way. The greater the number of words we can use properly, the wider the world ahead of us, and the better we feel. If our capacity to communicate is reduced, our unexpressed passions and desires sap our energy and, ultimately, our will to live. If, on the other hand, our capacity to communicate is well developed, our passions and desires sustain us.

Thankfully, it's easy for all of us to expand our active vocabulary. It's simply a matter of learning more interesting words and eliminating words with no precise meaning. The two go hand in hand: for every futile word we shed, we discover or rediscover others which are precise, strong and fruitful.

In practice, this involves asking ourselves, when we encounter a word that intrigues us, 'What does it mean to me? What *is* it to me?' and ignoring the tone in which it's spoken or the meaning others (second-rate dictionaries included) would have you ascribe to it.

Take the word 'politics', for example, which, as we know, is a conventional word – indeed, one of the most conventional of all.

Politics

What is politics? A person who is a *stupidus* in the Communication function might reply, 'Well, we all know what politics is. Everyone's always talking about it.'

Yes, but what is it?

'What is politics?! Well, it's what politicians do.'

And what do politicians do?

'Politics.'

I know people who would never escape this circular definition. I settled for it myself until the age of around fourteen, and at some points afterwards, too.

And yet, if you think about it (without searching for a definition online, which expressly *prevents* you from thinking about it), you will eventually come to the conclusion that the word 'politics' means 'dominion'. The aim of all politicians, in fact, is to have the chance to dominate other people.

'Politics', therefore, is a euphemism, since 'dominion' or 'domination' has negative connotations: I'm not likely to warm to, or want to hear about, or go out and vote for someone whose stated desire is to dominate people. But since that's exactly what a politician is, we have to conclude that the word 'politics' is imprecise, misleading and ought to be struck from our active vocabularies.

> QUESTION: 'But we need people to govern us. In that sense dominion, or domination, is necessary, isn't it?'
>
> ANSWER: 'Yes, that's the way the world works, for now. But then it's better to use the word "dominion" than the word "politics": it conveys more meaning. I could give you dozens of other examples of conventional words, and indeed I'll go on to list a few, but in the meantime, please, keep going. You have your common sense, which is all you need.'
>
> > COMMON SENSE: the innate ability to grasp the fundamental principles of knowledge, such as individual freedom, value and truth. It's the opposite of what the expression has come to equate: so-called good sense, which is the slowly acquired ability to reason along conventional lines.

Cleansing our personal lexicon has existential benefits, too, sweeping away layers of mental smog – provided we don't lose heart.

Indeed, having – perhaps with some amusement – struck a few imprecise words from our active vocabularies, we may stop looking for others, because discarding these words makes us stand out and feel isolated among the people around us who continue to use them. Standing out is wonderful, but feeling isolated is horrible, and the two are easily confused – today, more than ever.

Conformism is in the air, to an extent rarely seen over the past three centuries in the West. In conformist times, what is allowed to be said is the same as what the vast majority of people imagine they think, and what they want to hear. In other words, if communication is corrupted by words like 'politics', in the minds of most people that's absolutely fine. If this stands in the way of intelligence – causing, thereby, stupidity – nobody's going to make a fuss about it. And anyone who rejects the word 'politics' risks looking like an idiot, because they're going against the grain and saying things that sound strange to everyone else.

They don't even need to open their mouth: their behaviour, the look in their eye, the set of their lips, their silence, all their non-verbal communication will lead others to conclude that either this person is doing the wrong thing or everyone else is, and either way that person will be considered a pain in the neck. And nobody wants to be a pain in the neck.

This results in the following paradox: improving, enriching and cementing your communicative function has a detrimental effect on your social relations. When it comes to communication, we have a choice: be inwardly stupid, or appear to be a misfit; have nothing to say to ourselves, or give up all hope of being understood.

QUESTION: 'Isn't psychology supposed to help you solve your problems? This is a psychology book, but you're just creating more problems.'

ANSWER: 'Much of psychology aims to solve problems, and much of it ignores them. Neither of these approaches is the right one. What is a problem to you?'

QUESTION: 'Well, it's a setback, isn't it?'

ANSWER: 'A setback is a setback. The word "problem" comes from the ancient Greek *pro-* which means "forwards" and *blema* which signifies the act of throwing, hurling something a long way ahead of you. Having a problem means setting your sights or desires higher, or further, than usual. The Greek πρoβλημα was translated literally into Latin as *proiectum* – "project". Better not to "solve" or ignore one's plans and projects, but to take them seriously and allow oneself to be guided by them.'

SELF-DEFENCE

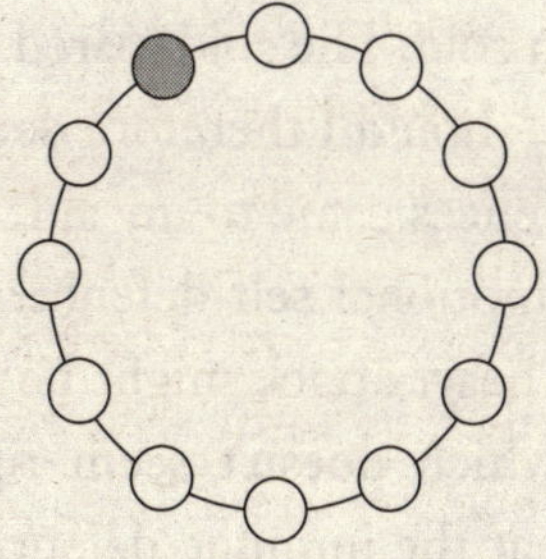

What exactly am I scared of?

It goes without saying that if you cannot defend yourself, you will face constant setbacks and thus be a *stupidus*.

There's physiological self-defence: the immune system. There's physical self-defence, which is the ability to avoid or contain conflicts with fellow humans or other animals. There's emotional self-defence, which means refusing to allow ourselves to be influenced by people or circumstances against our will. And there's intellectual self-defence, which is our protection from those who seek to impose their views on us, or to ridicule our own.

Sometimes it feels as though all of these aspects of self-defence are linked, and it's worth trying to understand how this might be so.

I once became unwell a few days before a social engage-
ment I hadn't been able to get out of: in other words, a
lack of emotional self-defence (I was dreading having to sit
through a conversation with people I didn't enjoy spending
time with, but couldn't bring myself to do anything about
it) went hand in hand with a drop in my immune defences –
I picked up a rotten cold. The cold spared me from having to
meet those people; should I therefore deduce that the drop
in my immune defences came to my aid, making up for the
weakness in my emotional self-defence? Probably not: by
that hypothesis, a heart attack might be considered a con-
venient get-out, which doesn't seem right somehow. I'd
rather conclude that the immune defences of timid people
are as weak as the other aspects of their Self-Defence
function.

One of the few times (pre-Covid) I've had a raised
temperature, I was due to take part in a theatrical performance. I went up on stage, and by the end of the show my
temperature had come back down to 36.2°C. The boost
to my emotional and intellectual self-defence from per-
forming was accompanied by a boost to my physiological
self-defence. I am, therefore, of the view that the various
aspects of the Self-Defence function are connected like
communicating vessels.

The Self-Defence function shapes and organizes the way we
see the world even more than Communication does: indeed,
it's our Self-Defence that defines what is real or unreal, possible or impossible to us.

REALITY: a vague term which dates back to barbarian (seventh century) Latin. I say vague because its meaning changes with the passage of time. For Dante's contemporaries, it was unrealistic to imagine that humans could fly, whereas nowadays flying is something we all take for granted; two centuries ago, magic carpets were a fantasy, but now we sit on aeroplanes with our feet on the carpeted floor. It's also common for reality and unreality to differ from person to person. For this reason, it's a good idea to use the word 'reality' in the plural ('realities') as far as possible, and to be wary of those who use it only in the singular.

It might be unrealistic for an actress making her debut to set her sights on an Oscar, but for another novice performer it might be an entirely different story: the first actress does not yet have the physiological, physical and emotional self-defence skills needed to navigate a series of ever greater successes, while the second knows she has these skills, or is capable of learning them; and the talent of both women (that is, the range of roles they are capable of playing) will depend solely upon this knowledge: one will fear success, the other will not.

Fear is, naturally, the *stupiditas* of the Self-Defence function, and calls for a little explanation.

Degrees of fear

The life we lead depends on the various degrees of fear we feel.

Most of the time, fear doesn't present itself in its most obvious form – shaking, irregular breathing and emotional and bodily paralysis – as a person with a fear of heights would experience peering over the edge of a ten-metre diving board. That would be first-degree fear.

Second-degree fear is more common: *the fear of fear*. The fear of fear is what leads a person with a fear of heights to swim in the pool without ever mounting the diving board, nor even stopping to look at it. They'll swim around happily, content with having ruled out the possibility of mounting the ten-metre diving board. Being fearful of fear allows us not to really experience fear.

If a third-degree fear arose in them, that is *the fear of the fear of fear*, they wouldn't even go to the swimming pool, because, if they did, they might find themselves tempted to wonder, 'What if I had a go at jumping from that diving board?' Those with a fear of the fear of fear do not experience the fear of fear, and have no idea what fear really is.

Third-degree fear is incredibly common: it limits our choices and is perceived as self-assurance. It shuts out areas of our brains and of the world around us, marking them off-limits. It gives us tunnel vision: out of fear of the fear of fear, apparently rational people organize their activities, their circle of friends, their topics of conversation and their hopes and dreams in a sort of network of narrow burrows, dug less out of the desire to achieve certain objectives than the need to escape many others, and to prevent the gaze from wandering freely. It takes a great deal of effort to hole ourselves up like this, but by force of habit it gets increasingly easier.

If their curiosity gets the better of them and they dare to peek out at the vast unexplored territories above them, or they hear talk of such places, third-degree cowards respond with nervous, bitter laughter (cracking inside their heads like a lion-tamer's whip) or disdainfully protracted vowels: 'Okaaay', 'Riiight'. So a person who believes in God (that is, a god without the indefinite article) is able to avoid all knowledge of polytheism, and a conservative all knowledge of anarchy – and that's down to the fear of the fear of fear.

But such imperviousness is nothing compared to the very many other things which provoke resistance in these people, but which they would be incapable of describing or even naming, having lost all knowledge of their existence. Thoughts that might have crossed their minds perhaps only once, as children, or things they have pictured in dreams, or heard, and feared, *and then forgotten*. All they remember – which is already sufficient to evoke the fear of the fear of fear – are a few feelings, or states of mind, or fragments of conversations that preceded or followed the thing which sparked fear and then fell from their minds.

So we might find ourselves unable to tolerate a perfectly kind and generous person, simply because their tone of voice reminds us of someone who came by that time we were thinking a terrible thought we can no longer remember.

Or watching a comedy, we might suddenly feel on edge,

because something in the frame recalls the room where we had that horrible dream which had already disappeared from memory the next morning.

I may never have succeeded in understanding integrals (and I haven't) because the maths teacher who first explained them to me walked the same way as the mother of one of my schoolmates, who had once somehow worried me in a way I can no longer explain (and never will). Third-degree fear plays these tricks on us: it is a prodigious inventor of *stupiditas*.

If only it served to train up our Self-Defence function. On the contrary, it weakens it. Third-degree fear diverts our Self-Defence towards minor dangers, which are too easily averted. When the only conflicts it ever encounters are easily resolved, our Self-Defence function, in all its guises, begins to consider real conflict insurmountable, and is stupefied, quickly throwing its hands up in defeat.

Across the centuries we have witnessed this grave consequence of the fear of the fear of fear in the majority of people. If the majority of Europeans had not allowed themselves to be weakened by their fear of the fear of fear, they could have avoided two world wars: the emotional and intellectual Self-Defence mechanisms of millions of adults would have stopped them, and physical Self-Defence would have prevented enlistment. But most of those adults shrank from being perceived as different – that is, they were unwilling to overcome the numerous cases of fear of the fear of fear which gave form to their conformism.

Improving one's own Self-Defence function ought not

to be difficult. It should simply be a case of increasing the number of second- and, ideally, first-degree fears we have, since these are the best antidote to those of the third degree. There are always plenty of things worth worrying about seriously.

Sadly, though, third-degree fear is fomented in every century by various religious and moral forces – all of which are equally vague about exactly what people are supposed to be scared of: the Devil, sin, divine disapproval, moral decline. And there are few places to hide from these forces: in a country where religion is much-discussed, even a committed atheist can't escape being conditioned by the dominant religion; in a country where morality is much-discussed, even an amoral person will have some scruples instilled in them.

QUESTION: 'So improving my Self-Defence also puts me at odds with others. Is this how it's going to go for the rest of the functions?'

ANSWER: 'Yes.'

A WORD OF WARNING ON PSYCHOLOGY AND SOCIETY

Developing the next ten functions also creates complications on a social level. Psychology must choose between promoting individuals' mental health and promoting their integration in the community: everyone who is sound of mind is an autonomous being with a will to understand, but if they want to fit in, they must obey a set of rules without asking too many questions.

In 1916, Jung put forward a commendable proposition:

> We could easily construct a political theory of neurosis, in so far as the man of today is chiefly excited by political passions to which the 'sexual question' [this was a dig at Freud] was only an insignificant prelude. It may turn out that politics are but the forerunner of a far deeper religious convulsion. Without being aware of it, the neurotic participates in the dominant currents of his age and reflects them in his own conflict.

Notice, though, the use of the conditional: 'We *could* . . .'

Jung subsequently decided he was better off leaving well alone and staying out of trouble.

In 1932, a prescient Einstein wrote to Freud asking him to rule against the inevitability of war: perhaps psychology might prove useful in preventing collective catastrophes. Instead, Freud replied that destructive impulses are natural, more so than the indignation they provoke in intelligent people, and therefore psychologists had no place interfering in the plans of warmongering politicians. This was a falsehood, given that the small number of destructive impulses within each of us is held in check by the far more numerous constructive and peace-loving impulses that war obliterates.

But psychology tends to prioritize fitting in above all else. There were a few notable exceptions in the fifties and sixties – Marcuse inspired the 1968 student movement, providing psychological arguments to support the protesters – but this was a brief window, after which the conflict between mental health and conformism (the healthier our mind, the freer we are, no matter how inconvenient or uncomfortable this might be) largely regained its taboo status.

It's a taboo we must break, because without it our analysis of stupidity would be incomplete and misleading.

QUESTION: 'So psychology is conservative?'

ANSWER: 'It depends. In states with a conservative majority, yes. In states with a progressive majority, psychology is also progressive.'

QUESTION: 'But what's the point in pitting my inner world against society? Individuals count for nothing these days. Other people are everything. A single person is just an addend; I have to find what I am meant to be added to. Why don't you just explain the rules of addition in society, and that'll do.'

ANSWER: 'The way I see it, the only way we can all be added together, or accumulated socially, is by losing ourselves. You can't combine addends of different types. One apple plus one orange doesn't make two. You can only add them together if you ignore what differentiates them – that is, by just calling them fruits: one fruit plus another fruit makes two fruits. The same goes for living beings: you can only add them together if you scrub out their identity; that is, if you forgo knowing precisely who it is you're talking about. Wanting to be like everyone else – in other words, addable – means being afraid of what we are, and this can become a third-degree fear, where you no longer know what it is you're actually afraid of.'

QUESTION: 'You really don't understand integrals, do you? Why don't you study them?'

ANSWER: 'I don't think that's the issue.'

EXTERNAL DIRECTION

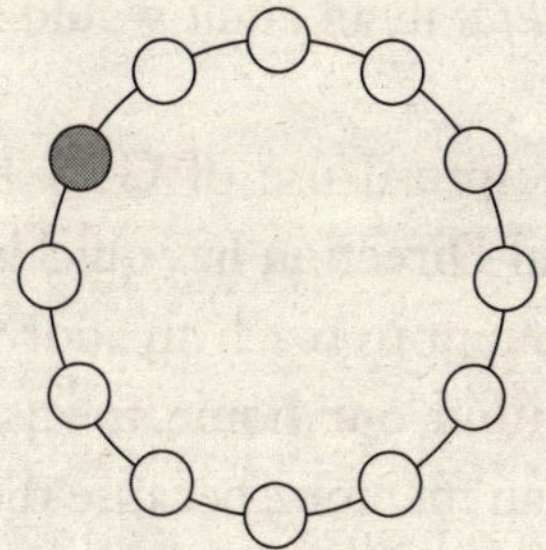

Am I still able to feel far away from anything?

External Direction is, above all, our ability to find our bearings in the *visible space* around us.

One hundred and fifty years ago, this was something very few of us could do: only a small minority of people travelled from place to place, and when they did, they relied on railways, ships or horse-drawn coaches, leaving the choice of route to the driver, captain or coachman. Most people only knew their way around their immediate surroundings; the rest of the world was the stuff of adventure-filled fantasy.

Twenty years ago, on the other hand, External Direction was highly developed: most of us either had a car or knew how to drive one, and could work out the best route along a comprehensive road network. Even the very young held maps of vast territories inside their heads. When we set off on longer journeys by train or aeroplane, we already had a clear sense of where we were going; news reports and documentaries helped us understand the physical and political geography of the planet, making the world feel smaller to us than it had to our great-grandparents. Twenty years ago, geographical *stupiditas* in an adult would have been considered pathological.

Today, the widespread use of GPS has created a new status quo. External Direction has quickly atrophied: many of us no longer attempt to reach an address without relying on satnav, even within our home towns. Maps are disappearing from human memory, because they're stored in the memory of our mobile phones.

Real damage has been done. Where once GPS was a mental prosthesis, it has become an everyday device for all of us, and the muscles of our External Direction are wasting in the same way as those in our legs would if wheelchairs came into fashion. At the same time, video calls have made the planet even smaller, not because we understand it better, but because understanding it doesn't seem important. The result is that our sense of spatial orientation falls ever further out of use.

One hundred and fifty years ago, no one would have believed that, with the march of progress, the visible space around us could have come to be considered so complicated that it took a mental prosthesis to get to grips with it.

'So how are these twenty-first century dwellers going to manage?' our ancestors might have asked. 'If they've ceased to understand distances, and can't even appreciate cultural differences – can't see that what's right in one place is wrong in another – what will they do?'

'It's true,' we would have to reply. 'We no longer understand that. Many people now think what's right for them is the right thing for all humanity.'

'So they're geographically stupid?'

'Yes, but wherever they are in the world, they'll be buying the same smartphones.'

External Direction also means being able to navigate professional decisions (finding a job, or in other words a *position*) and carving out a career (a term which originally indicated a type of road).

Here, things seem to be going better: our contemporaries are able to make well-informed decisions, career options have opened up massively, and compulsory schooling to the age of sixteen gives plenty of time for students to work out where their skills lie and what opportunities are available to them. Yet there is one worrying sign: the global rise of the Anglo-Saxon word *leadership*.

Leaders

In practice, what leadership means to workers is how to be the boss. There have always been bosses, always someone at the top, the capo or the head, and all that 'head' meant was 'the highest point in the landscape'. Dissecting the meaning of the word *leader* is far less simple: it's someone who leads others somewhere (the Italian equivalent would be the *duce* – who *conduce*, or conducts – and the German *Führer*).

But business leaders are not leading anyone anywhere; they're sitting behind a desk. So why adorn them with such a title, when others, such as 'director' or 'manager', would be more appropriate?

The use of the word 'leader' in business-speak is a symptom of a problem with the External Direction function. It gives the impression that those who answer to leaders are in need of assistance: 'Lead us, because we're lost. We spend every waking moment trying to escape the fact we have no idea where we're going, and we can't take it any longer.' The situation is serious.

Ultimately, the External Direction function concerns ideological choices.

In the realm of so-called 'politics' – in other words, in the relationships between people and centres of power – we also crave leaders. Since the start of this century, we have been going through a period of *who* – a period in which the question on most people's minds is 'Who?' and not 'What?', still less 'Why?' or 'How?'

The best periods are those in which the majority of people are not interested in knowing *who* matters so much as *what* matters, and thus also what some notable person or other – politicians, in particular – has done or plans to do. The most productive discussions, possible only during periods of *what*, are those around *why* and *how* a notable person has done or wants to do something.

Periods of *who* occur when the mental horizons of the majority of people are too narrow and troubled to accommodate the words needed to describe *what, why* and *how*.

The mind becomes a fissure wide enough only to hold a name and a face. And people are content with this: in elections, they vote for a *who*, rather than a party (which would be a *what*) or a political programme (which would be a *how* or *why*). In wars, they see a contest between two heads of state (two *whos*) or two peoples (another two *whos*), rather than a clash of two industrial systems (which would be two *whats*).

In periods of *who*, admiration for the occupant of a position of responsibility becomes veneration, disapproval becomes loathing, and people begin to believe that power is an innate virtue which can be used to explain everything, whereas power is only ever a consequence of collective dynamics. In periods of *who*, personal connections and endorsements count above all else; this has always been true of short-lived dictatorships, monarchies in decline and in certain ministerial departments, but in periods of *who* it becomes the general rule. And at times like these, the External Direction function is not only futile but almost totally irrelevant, because when it comes to External Direction, the *what* (places, distances, destinations) and *how* to get there are more important than *who* is giving directions.

Improving your External Direction is simple but physically demanding: it means walking (without looking at your phone). By walking, you gain a sense of distance and learn to look around you. As you do so, you realize there's a lot to see, and a great many things worth desiring – that is, things towards which the journey is more interesting and instructive. Things experienced at first hand, seen by your own eyes in three dimensions – unlike images seen online, taken and uploaded by others. Three-dimensional desires restore the impulsiveness, distinctiveness and tangibility to your External Direction function: suddenly you know *what* to head for and why – you, and only you, without relying on anyone else to guide you there.

The risk is that *what* you start desiring barely half an hour into your walk bears no resemblance to the life you have been living.

QUESTION: 'Isn't it greedy to want things all the time?'

ANSWER: 'Not in periods of *who*.'

INTERNAL DIRECTION

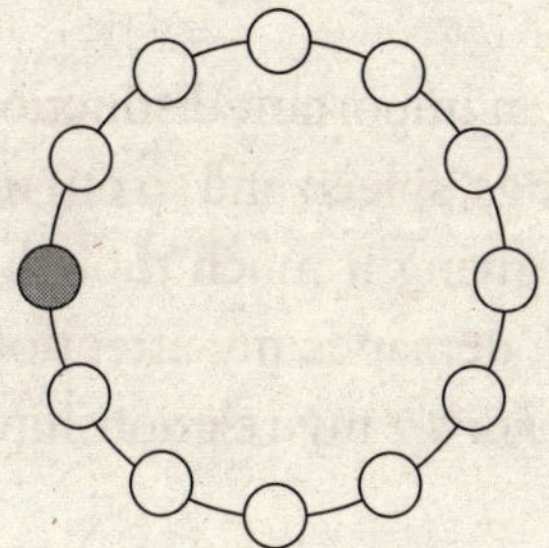

How many people seem mysterious to me?

Psychologically speaking, we are all amphibians. We live between two very different environmental states: one external, the other internal.

The first of these undoubtedly exists outside us. The second we imagine to be inside us, but there are reasons to doubt this. Inside me are groups of cells, nothing else, and it's not my cells I'm immersing myself in when I decide to shut myself off from the outside world. I'd have no idea what I was looking at, because I'm not a doctor or a biologist; I know so little about cells that my own are as foreign to me as the words of a person whose language I don't understand.

I prefer to take the term 'interior' as a derivative of the Latin *inter*, which means 'between'. As a matter of fact, my internal dimension is what lies *between* me and everything else – including between me and my body, and between me and the image I project of myself, and between me and who I think I am. This dimension of mine is not inside anything; it's not even inside me: rather, it's a place I can enter, in which I can immerse myself and spread out. I wouldn't be able to do that if it were inside me. Can a hand delve inside itself?

This strikes me as an important distinction to make: what is truly inside me (lungs, spleen and so on) mostly functions by itself, without my giving it much thought; my interior life, on the other hand, demands my attention both in order to *operate* and *not to obstruct* my relationships with the outside world.

It's up to me to make my 'interiority' operate: if I don't call upon my memory, my memory tells me nothing. If I don't listen to my sensations, my sensations remain silent, and so on and so forth. My interiority is a cognitive machine that requires an operator. If I don't use it, I am a *stupidus* in respect of my knowledge.

And it's up to me to stop my interiority obstructing me, or holding me back: if I don't know how to use it, everything I know becomes too vague. One of my favourite philosophers, Anaxagoras (500 BC), wrote:

What is hidden is revealed in what is shown.

In other words, the interior always has an obvious effect on the exterior, in the same way that the internal workings of today's movie cameras – the lenses, filters and angles – have an impact on the finished film. If I don't tend to my interior life, I will soon begin racking up a series of flops, and I will be a *stupidus*.

Those who cannot distinguish between the elements that make up their interior world will make poor or neglectful use of it. These elements are neither numerous nor complicated. I'll list them here:

> *Sensations*, that is, the information provided by the senses: sight, hearing, touch, smell, taste and telepathy (which is as much a sense as the other five, even if no dictionary admits it: we've all had the experience of sensing that someone was wishing us well or ill, even without having spoken to them for a while).

> *Memory*, which is another, interior, sensory system.

> *Feelings*, which select sensations, overlooking or distorting those which contradict their own narrative: the feeling of friendship for a person tends to blot out any unpleasant sensations aroused by that person, whereas the feeling of hatred blots out any agreeable sensations that person might arouse, and so on.

> *Emotions*: curiosity, anger, fear, playfulness, frustration, the desire to care for somebody, the desire to care for oneself, sexual desire, and so on.

> *Reason*, which is the ability to use acquired forms of logic recognized as useful by one's peers (what is considered rational and reasonable differs from one era to the next).

Morality, which is also acquired rather than innate, is a means of limiting and bending reason.

Thought, which is the ability to ask yourself 'Why?' and respond on your own terms, and which is almost always at odds with reason and morality.

Intuition, which is thought, on fast forward.

Imagination, which is the ability to describe in images or narratives what thought and intuition cannot explain.

Fantasy, which is the creation of images or stories for their own sake, and which is usually involuntary and innocuous.

Will, which finds its objectives by examining the activity of the other elements of the interior world.

None of these elements is unfamiliar to anyone over the age of seven (morality is fine-tuned at school, though we begin to build a sense of it even earlier than that). Every adult should therefore have long ago worked out how to distinguish between them, just as they can tell right from left, or differentiate between the points of a compass. In actual fact, most of us have a very thin sense of Internal Direction.

Many people confuse thought with reason, or even with morality: if they ask themselves or are asked 'Why?', they respond using acquired, preconceived and predictable forms of logic (thought, on the other hand, is never predictable). As a result, these people prove themselves stupid, but for the most part are too stupid to notice.

Some confuse imagination with fantasy: for example, they would say the *Divine Comedy* is a work of wild fantasy. In so doing, they miss the opportunity to use images to describe what their words cannot express – to them, they are 'mere fantasy'.

Others confuse emotions with feelings: for example, anger with hatred or sexual desire with love.

Many mistake feelings for sensations, giving rise to preconceptions.

Or they treat fantasy as if it were will – and end up in the perennial torment Catholics mistakenly call 'sinful thought', which involves repenting a flight of fancy as if it were a plan to be realized at the first opportunity.

And so on.

Forgetting

Our memory ought to be able to help us avoid such instances of internal disorientation: remembering the consequences of taking a wrong turn helps us avoid making the same mistake again. But memory is our least cooperative faculty, from the moment we first learn to forget.

Forgetting is a device small children learn as a way of tolerating the shortcomings of adults: they need to think highly of their parents, so they forget all the times their parents have disappointed them. It's easy. A child's memory is like a large room; forgetting the unpleasant things simply involves shoving them in a corner and never looking at them again.

It's a game, a test of our interior skills: 'If I manage not to remember that thing, I win; if I don't, I'll suffer.' All we've lost is a corner of our memory room. But unfortunately, precisely because it's so easy, the game tends to be replayed over and over: there are many disappointments we're better off forgetting, so the forbidden corners begin to multiply. As the years go by, our memory grows to the size of a palace, but much of it is off-limits. We can only tiptoe carefully around it in continual zigzags, and remembering the forbidden parts (that is, remembering to forget) becomes our principal mnemonic activity.

How can we forget to forget? In other words, how can we learn from others' mistakes and our own, to improve our Internal Direction and, therefore, our relationships with others (since we can't understand about other people what we haven't understood about ourselves)?

It's a question humanity has come up against since time immemorial, and the only satisfactory answer has always been: use what you have, including your interiority; take note of what you don't have and pursue it, look for it, find it. As we read in the great Gospel of Thomas:

> He who seeks should not cease seeking until he finds.
> And when he finds, he will be amazed.
> And when he is amazed, he will be dismayed.
> And then he will be king over all.

The Gospel of Thomas is a Middle Eastern text dating from the first century AD. In those days, there were many kings in the Middle East, and everyone talked about them. Everyone knew that kings had the ability to retain a great deal of information and manipulate it, or find their way around it. Being king or queen over all meant having no internal barriers, remembering not to forget anything. A dismayed king or queen is a nice image, one full of promise.

QUESTION: 'How am I supposed to look for what I don't have?'

ANSWER: 'Look.'

AUTHORITY

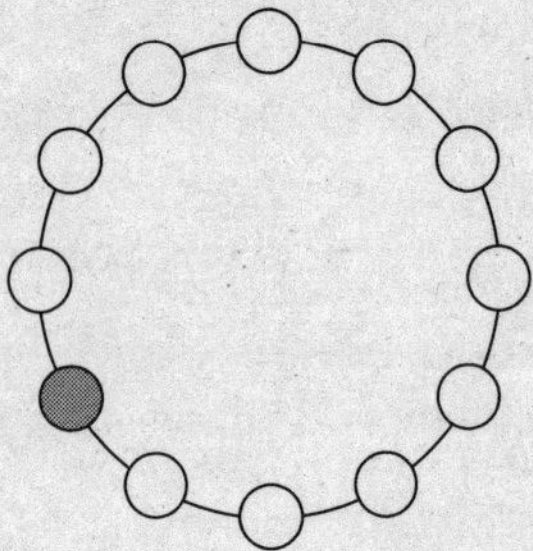

Am I certain of being right about something?

The Authority function pertains primarily to our personal authority. And personal authority is a matter of love. It's only worth making the effort needed to gain such authority if you care about other people. A famous example of this goes as follows:

> 'Who do people say I am?' [. . .] 'And you, who do you say I am?'*
>
> Mark 8:27–29

Jesus loved humankind and staked everything on his own personal authority.

* Here, as in the quotations from scripture throughout the book, the translations from the Greek are the author's own.

Another illustrious example is God himself. God wants to be the supreme authority in the universe, and his need for love is so great that he condemns those who don't love him to infernal torment.

Indeed, the love that is essential to authority is of the most passionate kind; a love not content to give and be given but that wishes to *take*. This grasping form of love demands approval, admiration, attention, dedication, gratitude, loyalty: these are the things authoritative people seek – and this is where their vulnerability lies, in comparison to those whose love is simply generous and given without expectation of anything in return. A grasping love puts its fate in other people's hands.

The Authority function also governs our reactions to other people's authority: that is, the ways in which we accept or decline offers of this demanding form of love from those who aspire to make subjects out of us – and there are always plenty of such people around. Our responses to these offers might vary between 'Why not, after all?', 'Fine, suits me', 'I thought you'd never ask!' and 'No, thank you'.

The tension between these two facets of Authority – exercising it or being subjected to it – is a constant of life in any society. One side always prevails as the other gives way, meaning that this function, unlike the others, cannot be inhibited by any means. In other words, no one is devoid of personal authority and free of the authority of others: in order to refuse any kind of authority, you must have decided to do so, and taking such a decision is an act of personal authority.

Thus the *stupiditas* here is not a question of lack in the function itself (an impossibility), but of distorting the love authority demands.

Rebellion

Rebellion is *stupiditas*.

People who rebel against authority believe they are doing so because they hate it, when really they just love it badly. Rebelling means trying to impose your own authority over someone else's. It's like saying, 'I won't give you the love you're asking for, and I'm going to force you to give me the love I want.'

It's surely a question of love, given that all it takes to destroy authority is to refuse it – just as one would spurn an unwanted admirer – and there are plenty of peaceful ways to do this, including criticism, protest and flight (sometimes an act of courage). Rebelling against an admirer means drawing them into a battle rather than letting them go. And we don't let go of the ones we love. So a rebel loves whatever form of authority they are fighting against, large or small. They seek its attention and think about it constantly. We could say that they live for it: if this authority were suddenly spirited away, they would no longer have a purpose; as long as it exists, they have a goal – as every eager lover does.

And the deluded rebel is invariably convinced of being in the right, contrary to the thing or person against whom their presumed hatred is directed. So their self-esteem is boosted, thanks to their adversary. They feel like a hero (we've all been there, if only by rebelling against a parent). Feeling heroic by virtue of someone else's wrongdoing is a pretty low trick, and one which often involves bending the truth: the more sordid the crimes I stand against, the better I feel about myself, and thus the more likely I am to exaggerate the gravity of those crimes, making me a *stupidus* in relation to the way things are, as well as in respect of my love.

Fanaticism

The other kind of *stupidus* in respect of Authority is the fanatic, whose behaviour is as absurd as it is predictable.

Fanatics are devout.

> FANATIC, from the Latin *fanaticus:* one who frequents the *fanum*, or the temple.

But they have devoted themselves – offered themselves – not to a god, but to a human figure of authority. They lovingly give of themselves entirely: the fanatic no longer makes their own decisions but simply obeys orders, and thus never feels responsible for their own actions. They do this either out of contempt for themselves, or out of contempt for the rest of the world: two forms of stupidity. And, once again, they're convinced they're right about everything.

The lessons of the Stalinist and Nazi horrors of the past century seem not to have been learnt. Fanaticism remains worryingly widespread, far beyond totalitarian states, terrorist organizations and sects. Every moralist wishes that all humans were fanatics and did only what that moralist believes to be right. Every religion forbids its followers from making their own minds up as to what is right and wrong. Every trend, every ideology, every tradition, every notion of progress demands subordination and promises a sense of superiority over all others. It's rare for anyone not to prove to be a fanatic.

The way to avoid rebellion or fanaticism is not to find a middle ground between asserting one's own personal authority and devoting oneself to another's authority (demanding a constant effort to avoid adhering to either extreme), but rather to embrace the pleasing solution which Virgil, in *The Divine Comedy*, offers Dante before bidding him farewell:

Thee o'er thyself I therefore crown and mitre

Purgatorio XXVII, 142

Meaning: I wish for you to be emperor and pope of yourself. In Dante's times, the imperial crown and papal mitre were the symbols of two supreme authorities: there was no higher power to submit to or rebel against in the world. Learn to discover these two forms of authority within yourself, Virgil says, thus pre-empting by almost six centuries one of the fundamental discoveries of psychoanalysis, the 'projection' mechanism. You project on religious and secular leaders a power that you have over yourself: use it. This power allows you to transcend yourself, to become, bit by bit, something bigger than yourself. When you feel like being right about something, try to get the better of yourself, put yourself in the wrong. Be devout or dare to be insubordinate to yourself, whenever you feel the need.

QUESTION: 'If people started following this advice, what would happen to all the kings and queens and popes?'

ANSWER: 'Nothing. They would carry on being obeyed by those who can't do without them.'

WEALTH

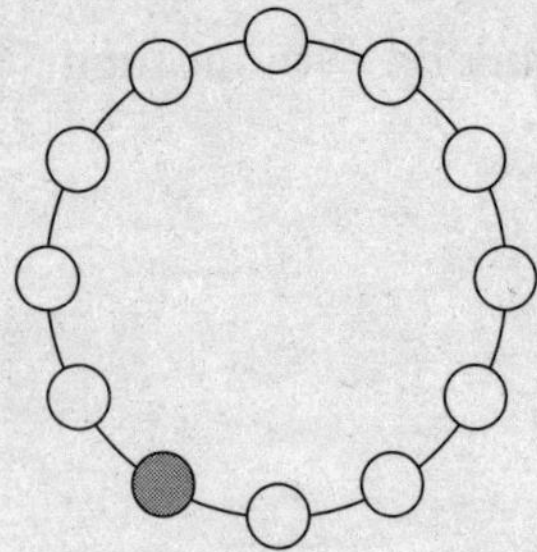

Do I want to work or *lavorare*?

Most of the time, we consider a person's wealth in terms of money. This strikes us as logical and necessary, given that everything we see and want comes at a cost.

But, as the saying goes, wealth is a state of mind; we would be richer in wisdom if we took wealth principally to mean our attitude towards abundance. This can be an abundance of anything:

of ideas;
of senses (sight, sound, touch, taste, hearing, telepathy);
of forces;
of time for ourselves (we can always find it, wherever we look);

of weak spots (to be acknowledged and overcome, in order to grow);
of curiosity, i.e. of potential questions and answers;
of faith;
of doubts;
of memories;
of ideals;
of desires;
and many other things above and beyond money.

Our wealth is the sense of the abundance we *afford ourselves* in any and all of these domains, and it depends exclusively on us. When this multifaceted, freely available wealth feels 'too much' (usually because someone who appears to know more than us has given us this impression), we distance ourselves from it, and instead put money at the top of our list of priorities. So we unconsciously place the highest emotional, spiritual, existential and even metaphysical value on money (as we measure the kindness of fate – a metaphysical entity – by the size of our bank balance), rather than on all this other wealth we can access gratis. On the one hand, since there will always be someone with more money than us, the result of this transfer of values is a sense of dissatisfaction. On the other, loading money with all of these other values only increases its psychological cost, or the psychological effort of earning it: it pushes us to sacrifice, one by one, the more beautiful forms of wealth listed above, for the sake of money.

This increase in the internal cost of money is the *stupiditas* of the Wealth function.

Facts

But – some will object – the fact is that earning money is a basic duty for all of us.

Yes, but even 'fact' is a conventional word. We believe, through hearsay, that facts are the cornerstones of reasonable argument, but the word 'fact' simply derives from the Latin *facere*: to do or to make. Someone makes or has made the facts we're talking about; they have selected certain pieces of information, impressions and memories from among billions of others, described them and ranked them in order of importance in our minds.

This someone is not God (God is only one fact) and not nature (nature is a collection of facts). The people who make all the facts are our peers, and the person who puts the finishing touches to these facts, making them seem noteworthy and definitive, is us: we choose, from among the numerous facts we're given, those which reinforce our certainties and bolster the decisions we take in our lives – such as the certainty that money is worth the sacrifices it's costing us.

Work

Words ought to help us evaluate facts: if we can describe a fact precisely, we should be able to assess how, why and by whom that fact has been devised and held to be important. Unfortunately, not every language contains the requisite words to form such descriptions, and in the Romance languages, there's a lexical gap when it comes to one of the essential areas of our Wealth function: work.

The work someone does to earn their living is a fact, but in Italian, French and Spanish, the words most commonly used to describe it have unhappy origins. Work is *travail* in French, *trabajo* in Spanish: both terms derive from *trepalium*, which in Low Latin referred to an instrument of torture. *Travail* and *trabajo* are also used to describe the pain of childbirth, like 'labour' in English. The Italian word for work, *lavoro*, derives from the same Latin root, *labor*, which signified 'hard toil'. No term in French, Italian or Spanish exists purely to signify productive activity that is carried out willingly and of benefit to all, like the English 'work', the Russian *trud* or the Hebrew *mela'ḳah* (which has the same root as *mal'aḳ*, 'angel', and *melek*, 'king'). Thankfully, this hasn't stopped a good many speakers of the Romance languages from finding fulfilling occupations, but they have done so *in spite of* the vocabulary available to them; had they taken the words at their disposal in earnest, they would have resigned themselves to seeing their *lavoro*, *travail* or *trabajo* purely in terms of struggle and sacrifice – as indeed many of their compatriots do, without imagining any possible alternative.

A well-developed Wealth function allows you to *spend the whole day* doing something you enjoy. On the other hand, when this function is underdeveloped, it leads to a betrayal of the self, in the same way Judas sold his future and his teacher for a derisory sum (thirty denarii, a tenth of the price of the ointment used to anoint Jesus's feet in John 12: 3–5). Learning to do better, resolving to stop selling yourself short, takes great courage. It means throwing away an entire life built on a *stupiditas*, along with the sorry image of the world and of destiny held up to justify it.

QUESTION: 'So why don't the Romance languages have a word for work done happily?'

ANSWER: 'I don't know. But these are three Catholic cultures and I think it has a lot to do with the papacy. The Roman Catholic Church is monarchical and rich, in the financial sense of the term, and monarchs and rich men don't spend a lot of time worrying about the happiness of working people.'

LEFT- AND RIGHT-SIDED FUNCTIONS

Since the late 1970s, Western science has known that the way in which the left side of the brain absorbs information and behaves is different from the right.

The left side of the brain is drawn to the contours of things, to distances, quantities and hierarchies. The right, on the other hand, is attracted to colours, contents and depths. When we look at a clock, the left side of the brain reads the time, while the right appreciates the graphic style of the numbers. For the left side, everything is exactly where it appears to be; for the right, the meaning of everything is also elsewhere. If they were two people, the left side would be wary of the right, and the right would be bored by the left. But they are two halves of a single organ, and so they work together.

I find this knowledge of the workings of the brain's hemispheres very pleasing, in part because it confirms the symbolic meanings attributed to left and right by some ancient cultures, and I've woven it into my theory of functions: Self-Defence, the two forms of Direction, Authority and Wealth are left-sided functions, neurologically speaking.

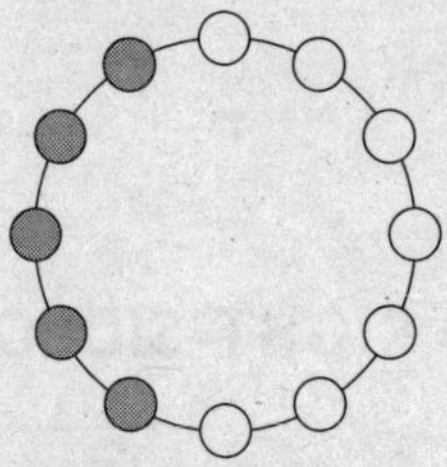

The next five functions we'll look at are right-sided, and they concern qualities and situations which might at first glance seem peculiar or irrelevant to a rational person. They are not. If they appear so, it's only because ours is a culture founded on the left side of the brain – with writing that goes from left to right and clocks whose hands would be going backwards if they moved from right to left.

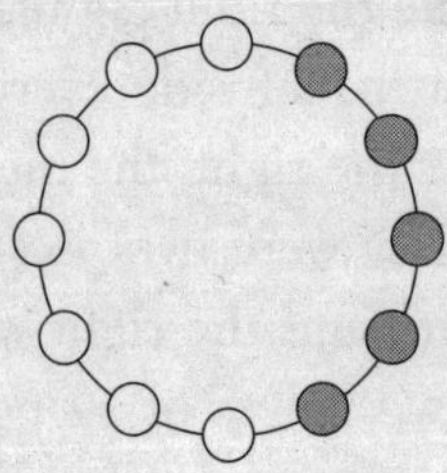

The other two functions, Communication and Attention, are dual-sided: Communication expresses and Attention observes what happens in both left- and right-sided functions. For this reason, they are placed at the top and bottom of the diagram, viewpoints from which they can survey the rest of the circle.

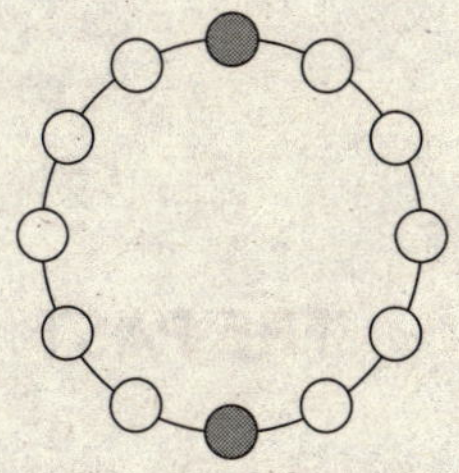

QUESTION: 'And is it possible to be stupider on the right side than on the left?'

ANSWER: 'Absolutely.'

THE PAST

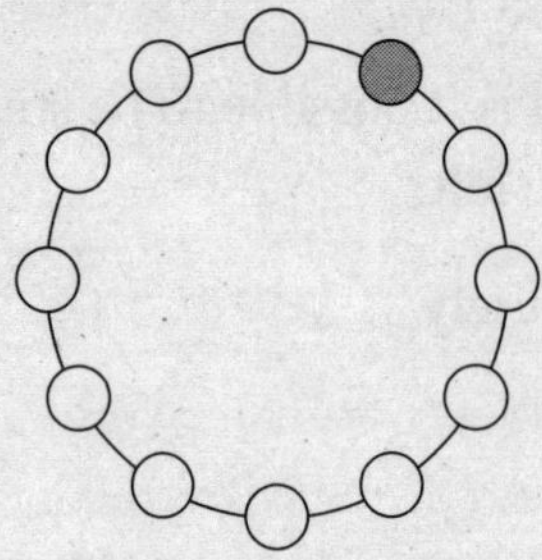

Am I still holding grudges?

From the late eighteenth century, our civilization began to look down on its own past. Kant declared confidently in 1784 that Enlightenment, the philosophical movement in fashion at the time, was 'humanity's emergence from a state of immaturity': inhabitants of previous eras were thus considered juveniles.

During the nineteenth century, these pretensions only grew bolder. Not only fashionable philosophers but practically all modern Westerners viewed the past as inferior to the present, legitimizing efforts to rid the world of peoples whose culture was considered backward: Native American and Aboriginal people, among many others. The driving force was no longer the criminal fury of conquest, as it had been three centuries earlier in South America, but the conviction that 'modern' meant 'better', and anything unmodern was an obstacle to be swept aside.

This same conviction lasted into the twentieth century. Bolshevism destroyed the old regime and the tens of millions who didn't hate it enough; Nazism sought to wipe out the Jews, whose culture was the most ancient in Europe.

Those of us born after the Second World War are heirs to this long-held historical obtuseness. For a while, we managed to shrug it off to some degree, by reappraising ancient cultures – American Indians, Vikings, Anglo-Saxon mythology in Tolkien's retelling, the Egyptians – and viewing them with newfound admiration. But historical short-sightedness and disregard of the past is returning, and the events of recent centuries in particular are disappearing from view: it's rare to meet anyone who has watched Rudolph Valentino's films or who knows anything about Garibaldi's conquests.

These cultural deficiencies reduce not only our potential topics of conversation but also the number of problems we encounter on a daily basis – which some would consider a boon, and others a matter of great concern.

A short historical memory is a good thing, according to some, because every era has its own problems and develops the skills needed to solve them. There is no shortage of problems facing us today, and thus no need to go digging up others from centuries past which would only cause a distraction. We should keep ourselves to ourselves, 'cultivate our own garden', as Voltaire wrote in the last line of *Candide*.

QUESTION: 'Voltaire? Who's that?'

ANSWER: 'One of the grown-ups I was telling you about at the beginning of this chapter.'

The limited scope of our historical memory is a serious issue, say others, for the same reasons: our problem-solving skills are engaged with current issues, making us overlook the problems of the past – but, as we saw earlier, 'problems' are not so much setbacks as potential new outlooks. Thus, those who limit themselves to cultivating their own gardens are missing out on the many perspectives the past could offer them.

The problems/perspectives of the past still have the potential to shed light on the future. An actor could learn more from the way Rudolph Valentino behaved in front of the camera than by watching a Tom Cruise movie. Garibaldi's successes and failures help us to understand Italy better than this morning's newspapers can. And every great leap forward has gained its momentum and meaning from a context that came long before it.

Saint Francis of Assisi drew inspiration from Jesus, taking problems and existential discoveries dating back twelve centuries and adapting them to his own times.

Jesus had drawn inspiration from the perspectives of Elijah and Moses, who lived respectively nine hundred and something like twelve hundred years before him:

two men were speaking with Him: they were Moses and Elijah

Luke 9:30

And Moses drew inspiration from the perspective of Abraham, who lived who knows when.

Einstein took a new approach to one of Newton's theories, as if that theory had been formulated only the week before.

Freud established psychoanalysis by rethinking the age-old practice of interpreting dreams and revisiting the Greek myths.

Jung took seventeenth-century alchemy seriously. And in 1958 Popper—

QUESTION: 'Who's Popper?'

. . . Popper advised philosophers and scientists to go back to the pre-Socratics. And so on.

QUESTION: 'The pre-Socratics . . . is that a sort of political party?'

ANSWER: 'They're the philosophers who came before Socrates. And Popper was a philosopher of science.'

Just as exploring the distant past can lead to philosophical and scientific advances, it can also help us progress on an individual level. Reading about the Greek gods and their messy, passionate ways, or the Egyptian gods with their fantastical animal heads, brings with it a number of unforeseen advantages: upon closing the book, people we previously found objectionable might begin to seem interesting; something that once provoked insecurity and resentment might come to feel insignificant; situations we believed closed might show newfound potential. All this because a better relationship with the past broadens our perspectives.

This positive effect can also be explained in neurological terms: many of our uncertainties derive from over-development of the skills controlled by the left side of the brain, which are firmly rooted in the present moment; ancient religions, on the other hand, stimulate the skills of the right side of the brain, which allow us to see beyond Voltaire's 'garden' (which is a form of *stupiditas*), to take inspiration from a range of sources and seize new opportunities.

Some might protest that the distant past is 'on the right' in a different sense: in centuries and millennia past people were more aggressive; slavery existed; Hitler revived the Aryan myths.

Starting with Hitler, let's be clear: he didn't revive anything at all. Nazi ideologies simply invented subjects for propaganda purposes: the Aryan race had never existed. As for the rest, no one can claim that the past was better than the present, just as they could never demonstrate that ancient Greek is better than modern English; the ancients simply talked about things we no longer discuss. These things have fallen from view because the past is behind us, and not because our contemporaries are now able to see things more clearly.

Even Aladdin's lamp once lay forgotten and covered in dust. Bringing it back into the light of day and making use of it means evading the rule of the most stupid of masters: time, as our Western civilization conceived of it – as a hermetically sealed capsule of the present moment, which only moves forward along a single line at the constant speed of one per hour, leaving everything behind. This concept of time is also a convention.

Time

From the Greek *temnō*, meaning 'to divide'. The word 'time' simply indicates a way of dividing *something* into years, days, minutes and seconds; there is no word to indicate that *something* that time is dividing up, which remains an unsolved X in the equation.

Whatever this X is, it is a concrete thing, whereas dividing it up as time is an abstract operation. And yet time is imposed upon us as the most concrete of realities: if it's now 12.26 p.m., it cannot and must not be 11.09 a.m. And what's in the past is in the past, and those who are no longer with us are no longer with us – not because this is truly so (we don't know what this X is, so we have no idea what's possible or impossible within it) but purely because the abstraction we call time would otherwise be a matter of renewed debate. The reluctance to redebate an abstraction is another form of *stupiditas*.

The abstraction we call time forces us to believe that a memory is nothing but a memory, and so to consider the opportunities that might have been offered by past eras as irredeemably lost. This rings ever more suspiciously, and begs the question: who benefits from making us uphold this abstraction called time? Only those who give out orders, in any given area, and those resigned to following them: two categories of people who hate debating anything.

If, on the other hand, we were to discover that our

recollections meant something more, that our memories were not archives but sensors, and that inside this X, everything was still there waiting for us, within reach, imagine how much richer life could be for those who don't wish to belong to either of those two categories of person.

Thus Borges, quoting Rhett Butler without undue irony, wrote that a gentleman has a weakness for lost causes, once they're really lost.

QUESTION: 'Who's Rhett Butler?'

ANSWER: 'The one from *Gone with the Wind*. Haven't you seen it?'

QUESTION: 'Oh, him. And which one was Borges?'

YOUR PAST

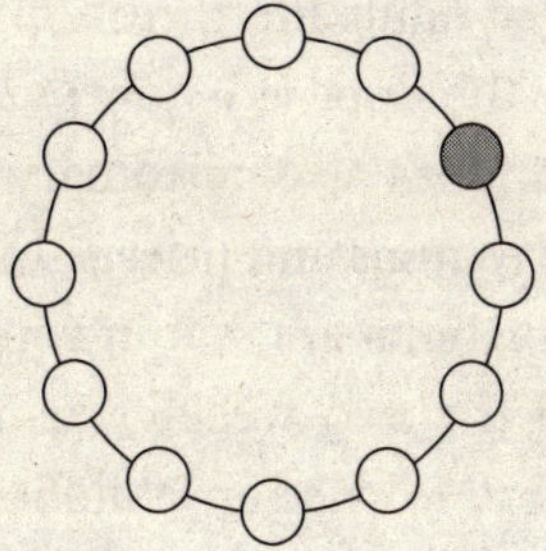

Do I still talk about myself differently
from how I talk about others?

Our relationship with our own past is at the root of psychoanalysis: patients are encouraged to remember their childhood as they lie on the therapist's couch. Psychoanalysis does not, however, promote a *good* relationship with our past: it considers childhood and puberty as phases best put behind us, and views children as mini delinquents fortunately not yet wily enough to act upon their constant urges – homicidal hatred for one parent, sexual desire for the other. Freud must have really loathed children.

Yet a good relationship with our past selves is exactly what this next function of the right side of the brain aims to achieve – in its spanning beyond the bars of the present moment.

Catholicism can consider itself a master of this particular art. It understands that the inner wellbeing of the faithful depends, to a large extent, on retaining the links to the past that the demands of adult life threaten to sever. Catholics are expected to see the Pope as a holy *father* and the Church as a holy *mother*, and it's also customary to give the names mother and father to nuns and priests. In this way, Catholic parents and grandparents are still in some way able to feel like children. And the two weekly sacraments, confession and communion, are learned in childhood, allowing adult believers to continually relive something of that time.

A cynic might say this is simply a way for the Church to exercise control over its members: if you keep people feeling like children, they'll keep obeying as they did in childhood. That's missing the point – and besides, children are generally far less obedient than adults.

Any self-respecting adult endeavours, mostly through fear, to forget and distort the memory of their own childhood. If they listened to what it had to tell them – that is, if they judged themselves through the eyes of their nine-, six- or four-year-old self – they would struggle to maintain any sense of pride; too much of their own daily behaviour would seem foolish, pointless, cynical or reckless. Better instead to treat children as silly and naive, with their insistence on always asking *why*. 'As if there were any need to know why!' grumbles the adult.

The Church, on the other hand, wants its followers to ask questions about everything, as children do. The trouble is the Church then provides a series of handy ready-made responses through the catechism, and other similarly prescriptive answers through its teaching. And yet our relationship with our own past is only truly good and fruitful if it allows us to rediscover the questions we asked in childhood *to which we are yet to find an answer.*

The questions children ask are simple and concrete, and concern the most obvious aspects of our existence. This makes them of fundamental importance.

Our unanswered questions reach out beyond the confines of our intellects and invite us to follow their lead.

Simplicity and intellectual courage are what make children's questions so brilliant. And brilliance is what we need most, at the best and worst moments of our lives. To give an example:

'Why do people get married?' our infantile curiosity might wonder, if our relationship with our own past is good.

'Two people get married because they want to be together,' our adult mind might reply.

'But weren't they already together before getting married?'

'Yes, but getting married is just the done thing.'

'Why is it the done thing?'

In the space of three moves, the adult is already in check. There is only one option left for the adult mind, and it's a weak one. It replies: 'Because if they're married, it's harder for them to break up when they fall out of love.'

'But if they fall out of love, why should it be hard for them to break up?'

Checkmate.

For an adult mind, losing a game against infantile curiosity means breaking down at least one convention you have thus far blindly followed out of *stupiditas*. It's one of the worst moments in life, because of the realization that you didn't need to be beholden to this idea for so long: you could have simply asked, 'Why?' Yet it can quickly move on to become one of life's best moments, when you realize you are beholden no longer. There are few things more desirable.

In order to develop a good relationship with our own past, we must once again conjure it up like the genie in Aladdin's lamp, descending into the cave (or cellar) of our memories, dusting off what might at first seem like mere bric-a-brac. Looking at old toys and photos and telling ourselves, 'I was there; I was like this.'

Through remembering our childhoods, verbs in the past tense undergo a transformation that confuses our rational mind and even temporarily blocks our left-sided abilities: the imperfect, the present perfect, the simple past all give way to the infinitive – 'I was like this' becomes 'to be like this'.

The grammatical infinitive

The infinitive is one hell of a tense, grammatically speaking. It simultaneously expresses a desire, a possibility, an achievement, a plan of action and, as an imperative, an order to oneself: *be like this!* It's called the infinitive because it indicates actions or situations that are open-ended, that haven't ended and may never end: this is precisely the extra-temporal dimension in which our personal memories reside – as long as the left side of our brain allows us to reach them.

That little girl is not only who you *were*; you might still *be* that girl, just as you can also be the teenager or twenty-something you once were, or the woman you are today. It's for you to choose; don't limit yourself.

Lastly, a tactical error that can ruin everything, in respect of our relationship with our own past, is the belief that our own childhood is incomparable to anyone else's.

It's an easy mistake to make, because our experiences may well seem unique to us, which is why it takes supreme reserves of patience to sit through another person's account of a holiday they once took – unless that other person is Marcel Proust. But the banal narcissism of memory robs our childhoods of the chance to play an active role in the world: if you think of something as solely yours, that's how it will be, and a state of seclusion will follow.

Far better to remember that we once looked at the world and asked, 'Why?' in the same way everyone else did. Thus the benefits of a good relationship with our own past can be shared with every other adult who allows themselves to be a child, opening up a new common language and bright sense of solidarity.

QUESTION: 'Won't I seem a bit ridiculous if I start feeling like a child?'

ANSWER: 'Perhaps. But then again, in this day and age, it's impossible to be more ridiculous than an adult.'

OUTSIDER

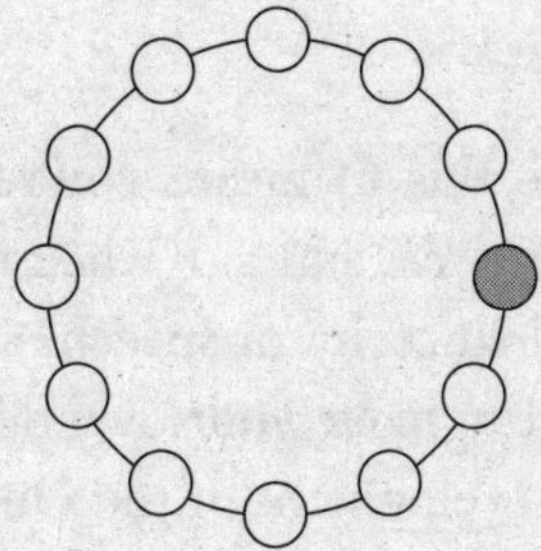

Do I still feel lacking in energy?

The primary goal of not just American psychology but psychology as a whole is to help individuals to integrate into their community and share the values of their people.

It's therefore common for psychologists to excuse, as inevitable, certain less-than-honourable expedients to which people resort in order to fit in: envy, which binds us to others more than anything else; duplicity, which helps us avoid conflict; cowardice, which prevents us from having to make choices we would struggle to explain to others. We can justify envy by calling it competitiveness, duplicity by calling it politeness, cowardice by calling it loyalty – thereby transforming all three into social virtues.

Arguing for the need to integrate into various groups (starting with one's own family and moving progressively upwards from one's primary-school class to society as a whole) essentially means going against the Gospel exhortation not to pledge allegiance to anybody:

> 'Instead, may the way you speak be: "yes" when it is yes, and "no" when it is no.'
>
> Matthew 5:37

We should take this to mean: you're better off saying 'yes' when it's yes *for you*, and 'no' when it's no *for you*. This kind of clarity and sincerity of speech, and the courage to fight for your right to make your own decisions, goes hand in hand with the development of the Outsider function.

Those with weaknesses in the Outsider function have a limited type of presence in the world: they occur, you perceive them, they *are*, but they do not *exist*.

> TO BE means occupying a place within a specific space, environment or group. 'I was' means I was in that spot. Everyone *is*, in some way or another. TO EXIST (from the Latin *ex*, 'outside' and *sistere*, 'to stand firm') means to emerge, stand out. We exist in the proper sense when we differentiate ourselves from others.

Consequently, a good synonym for Outsider is 'existent'.

'Do I exist?' This question is the starting point from which the Outsider function develops. Most of the time, the answer is 'no' – until a moment of great joy, an illness, some serious, notorious mistake, or death, forces us to exist a little, at least for a while. Because existence is frightening. When you exist, you are seen: others notice your strengths (which may be few), along with your weaknesses (which may be many). We feel safer when we pass unnoticed, when we're able to blend into a crowd, be among our people: peoplehood is the refuge of the *stupidus* of the Outsider function.

But 'people' is just a conventional word.

The people

We often talk about 'the people', and because of this, we not only believe we all know what it means, but we also imagine it denotes something real.

This is doubtful, firstly because this 'people' is always somewhere else. It should be nearby, but is there a place where you can see it? Not that I know of. In a shopping centre in the run-up to Christmas, at the beach or in a traffic jam on the motorway in July, in the town square during a major demonstration, it's not a people we can see, only lots of other humans, each of whom might perhaps imagine the others to constitute the people. Some speak highly of their people and are proud to be a part of it; some go so far as to love it, thereby putting into practice the first and most basic instruction given to us to convince us that peoples exist:

'You will love your neighbour as yourself'

Leviticus 19:18

This is the instruction Moses gave to the thousands of refugees he was guiding towards the Promised Land.

He wanted to keep them united, wanted to make a people out of them, give them an exclusive national identity – an idea that was completely foreign to them. These refugees had been born and raised under the Egyptian empire, and there is no concept of peoplehood in empires, because the ensuing demands for autonomy would prove troublesome to emperors. So Moses had to explain this new concept in a way his followers could understand. He succeeded: being a people – he so famously said – means loving *those close to you* (that is, your neighbour) and not those who are far away, and loving them as you love yourself. On the one hand, this gives impetus to those who hate empires (which encompass populations spread over vast territories); on the other, it unfortunately also provokes hatred of those who believe in the parity of all humans, near and far. And yet Moses' formula won out: still now, belonging to a people means being less inclined to care about billions of others, simply because they're a long way away.

But the most striking thing about Moses' exhortation is the contradictory affective effort it demands: it dictates a feeling that would be worth something only if it was spontaneous: *Thou shalt love!* Is it possible to love on command? And to love only one person (your neighbour) and not another (distant) person in this way? Only if the word 'love' becomes another conventional word bearing no resemblance to what love truly means. And yet, to this day, the existence of a people rests solely on this effort, intuited by Moses, to love one's compatriots more than foreigners: and so what we have here is a conventional object, a people, brought into existence through a conventional form of affection, an assumed and preordained feeling. And that doesn't amount to much.

Yet this 'love', invented and broadcast by Moses thousands of years ago, ends up binding the individual to a majority with profound ties. When we love someone, we care about what they think of us; we want to please them, we want them to be happy with our behaviour and our choices. In short, we become dependent on that someone – which is beautiful when love is authentic and in full bloom but not when it is a conventional and mandatory sentiment.

The development of the Outsider function pushes one to distance oneself from the idea of 'people', as it proves too costly in terms of personal energy and the will to live: it costs us to conform to the many prohibitions, duties and permissions established by a majority, justified only by the claim that 'this is how it is done among our people'. Of course, it's nice to win the approval of our peers, from time to time. But when it happens, we can't help but wonder, 'Do they approve of me because what I'm doing suits them more than it suits me?' and we find ourselves wanting something different.

The more we really exist, the more energy we have, and as we regain the will to live and do, our energy is boosted even further. As for our need for approval, the way to get around it without causing offence is with simple good manners.

QUESTION: 'Good manners?'

ANSWER: 'Gentle irony.'

A NOTE ON IRONY

An ironic attitude serves not only as a form of politeness protecting the outsider from entering into open conflict with the world of convention (irony ensures a place for everything, for my way of thinking as well as yours – and it does so with a smile); it is also the only good way for those with a solid Outsider function to approach thinking about anything, including themselves.

In this difficult phase in the history of our civilization, *nothing is as it was*, and *nor is it yet as it will be*. Whatever value you put on anything (traditions, innovations, compromises, institutions, alternatives) is anachronistic; it's already a decade out of date, belonging to a time before today's wars and before Covid, and it may soon vanish completely. At times like these, we have two options: either we try, through *stupiditas*, to convince ourselves that nothing has changed, or we give ourselves permission to feel freer than we did before.

Those with a good relationship to the Outsider function are able to enjoy this sense of freedom, which is a freedom even from themselves; in a transitional world, there is no point in clinging to an idea of oneself that will soon be superseded. This unburdening allows the mind to be incredibly agile, proving that everything we know is only *what little we know now*, which will soon be nothing but dead weight; and nothing lightens the load better than an ironic joke, provided it's a good one.

Those of a serious disposition might be under the impression that ironic people don't believe in anything, and therefore don't love anything. This is not true. We love most deeply that which we don't yet have. Irony loves the future that lies ahead, undiscovered, and loves in all of us what we might one day become. The deep reserves of energy tapped by a solid Outsider function are what make this outpouring of love possible.

QUESTION: 'What if I don't want to make ironic jokes about myself?'

ANSWER: 'Then you're the ironic joke.'

SENSE OF OBSTACLES

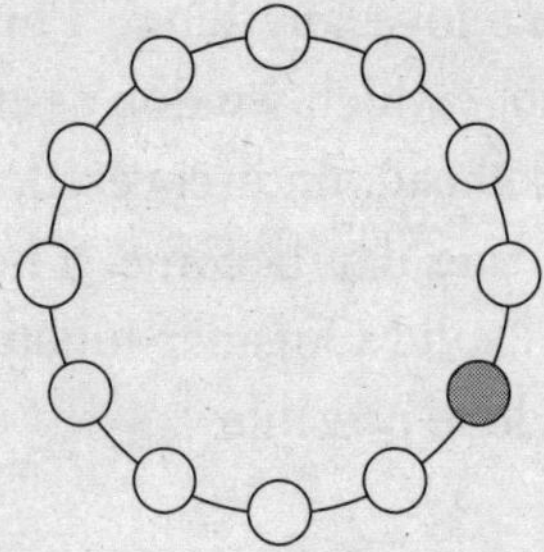

Do I still struggle to set myself new goals?

The Sense of Obstacles is a highly counter-intuitive function – that is, it goes against what the majority of people imagine themselves to intuit naturally. The word 'sense' is used here to mean taste, inclination, sensibility. We might describe someone as having a sense of style or of justice if they couldn't do without style or justice for prolonged periods of time. But most people – other than athletes, poets, philosophers and the best theoretical scientists – do without obstacles quite willingly.

Athletes can't do without difficulties in their sport, and they compete to break records, which represent the main obstacles standing in their way.

Poets, if they are truly poets, write what has previously been considered too difficult to express.

Philosophers (not historians of philosophy, who are another breed entirely) overcome obstacles which have previously prevented their colleagues from grasping and explaining something.

The best theoretical scientists consider all theories preceding their own as obstacles, and thus the ultimate purpose of any scientific theory is to be rendered obsolete.

The approach to difficulty taken by these scientists, athletes, poets and philosophers is at odds with that of the technical advances cherished and celebrated by so many. Technical advances aim to reduce the number of obstacles we face, to make our lives as easy as possible. The washing machine made it easier to do the laundry, the computer made it easier to calculate, Park Assist sensors made it easier to park. Progress-lovers want nothing more than to sit back and relax in comfort, and have fewer desires than those who set themselves challenges and are always looking for more. The former aspire to be increasingly content; the latter are happy to aim for a happiness that is always just out of reach.

This might seem like a strange kind of happiness: being happy not to be happy yet, nor perhaps ever. But it does make a kind of sense: for those who have developed their Sense of Obstacles, settling for things as they are is a sign of defeat, whereas every problem presents the opportunity for adventure and invention, for acts of creation – a pursuit shared by some gods.

Yet having a Sense of Obstacles is not an option reserved only for the few. Anyone waking up to their own abilities can feel its effects. As we grow, we find obstacles and confront them. The only way to stop growing is to stop finding obstacles – that is, to be stupid in respect of obstacles.

And, thankfully, anything can present an obstacle to those who are growing: as we grow, we change, and every change overcomes a hurdle, extends the limits of our wants and needs. There is no certainty we cannot end up doubting, no ideal we won't eventually consider a constraint. And for this reason, politicians, religious figures and leaders of all shapes and sizes try to manipulate individuals' Sense of Obstacles because they fear being left behind. Those who wish to dominate other people say, 'The only obstacles you can face are the ones I tell you to have, and if there are others you've set your sights on overcoming, that's because you're pretentious, and they don't really count.' This is an inducement to *stupiditas* and exploits a very common problem which has been the subject of countless psychological studies: groupthink.

Groupthink

Since the 1970s, groupthink has been classed as a mental dysfunction. It is characterized by the belief that you can only belong to a particular group if you impede your own ability to identify difficulties and obstacles that other members of the group haven't recognized. In this sense, therefore, groupthink maintains a level of *stupiditas*.

For example, during mass, when the priest directs everyone to recite the Pater Noster, he knows that what's written in the Gospel according to Matthew is not 'Give us this day our daily bread' but

panem nostrum supersubstantialem da nobis hodie,

meaning 'give us today, immediately, our food of the world above'. The priest knows this, because he studied Latin at the seminary and has certainly read the Gospel, but he doesn't highlight the discrepancy, because it would lead to confusion and irritation among the group of people in front of him (his parishioners), and would undermine the authority of the Roman Catholic Church, which approved this erroneous translation. The same could be said of a Protestant pastor or an Orthodox pope, since the error is found in all versions of the same prayer, whether in Italian, English, German, Spanish or the Slavic languages. This mistranslation is not inconsequential. There is quite some difference between asking God to provide our daily sustenance and asking Him to grant us immediate access to eternal energy sources: in the first case, God becomes a god of fortune; in the second, He is the god of spiritual and existential evolution. But groupthink dictates that we continue to play dumb.

Psychologists mostly study the impact of groupthink in business, politics and familial contexts, where it can do a great deal of damage. Information that risks undermining the integrity of the group is distorted. People are reluctant to express differing points of view. They fail to identify objectives and risks that have been overlooked by other members of the group, and they experience the loss of identity that is typical of fanaticism, as we have already discussed. In this way, the group itself becomes the true obstacle, but its members are always reluctant to admit it.

How many groups do you belong to?

In other words, to what extent are the weaknesses in your Sense of Obstacles, the hindrances to your existential growth, caused by various forms of solidarity?

It's always worth asking ourselves this question. Personally, I'm convinced that these forms of solidarity are the main cause of our *stupiditas* in relation to obstacles; obstacles which have done, and will continue to do us, so much good.

QUESTION: 'So when I watch the athletics on TV, do I also get this feeling of being happy to be unhappy you were talking about?'

ANSWER: 'Yes.'

QUESTION: 'Is that why so many of us enjoy watching it?'

ANSWER: 'Exactly.'

OVERCOMING OBSTACLES

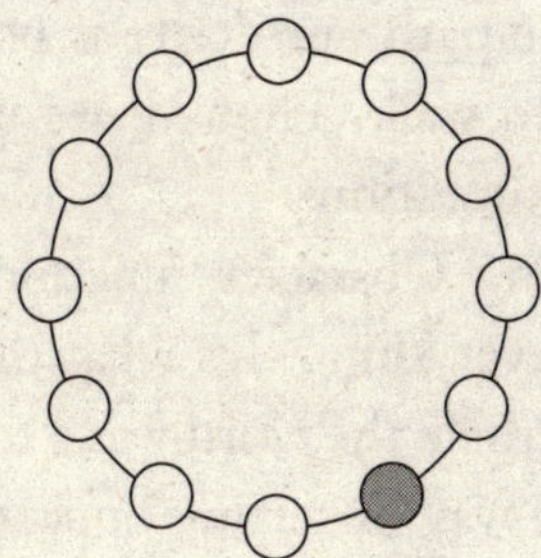

Do I have or seek obstacles that daunt me?

This function relies on being comfortable with the idea that every obstacle can be overcome – and that obstacles are not, therefore, to be feared.

For example, it means sensing (whether as sensation or feeling), *before asking a question*, that we might already know the answer, however difficult that question might seem: each question we ask simply expresses what we were already on the verge of revealing to ourselves – otherwise we wouldn't have thought of asking that precise question among the billions of others we might pose at any moment.

The same goes for desires, even those which appear impossible to fulfil. Desires are another form of question, directed towards the future: 'I want that thing' means 'Will

I have, will I do that thing?' And if wanting that thing makes us smile – not, as it may seem, out of fondness, but rather out of joy (a sure sign that the desire is authentic) – then this particular thing, among billions of others, has attracted us precisely because it is close at hand, within our grasp, lying just ahead of us on one of the many paths our future might take us – the path our desire is pointing us towards and preparing us to walk. Then all we need do is trust in our desires, or our questions.

The Overcoming Obstacles function means believing in oneself and in everything. It's what the early Christians called 'faith'. Back then, the word was a technical term connoting a particular way of seizing opportunities with more speed, daring and, often, more precision than was possible through the powers of reasoning and thought (later, in the language of religion, the word 'faith' came mostly to indicate a form of groupthink, meaning unconditional allegiance to a doctrine and the authority promoting it). So, in the Gospels, 'ye of little faith' are those with weaknesses in Overcoming Obstacles.

A poor relationship with this function is usually caused by a lack of this 'faith' or trust. The only hope is that those who suffer from this *stupiditas* also have a low Sense of Obstacles, because even the slightest obstacle will seem insurmountable to them: the fewer of them they have to face, the less frustrated they will feel. They will succeed in leading the life of a barnyard animal: all habits, no surprises. When trouble arrives on the farm, they'll wait for it to pass (this too shall pass) and place their trust in their own resilience.

The famous resilience

The word 'resilience' has been widely misinterpreted in recent years. It is taken as a virtue to be encouraged, and used in this sense in psychology texts, journalism and ministerial decrees. But the word 'resilience' actually refers to the elasticity that allows an object to regain its original shape after being compressed: a rubber ball is resilient, a ping-pong ball is not. Applied to human beings, 'resilience' suggests an unwillingness to embrace change after emerging from a difficult situation: following a setback, a resilient person goes back to behaving exactly as they did before. This is not a virtue, but a sure-fire way to waste opportunities for growth.

It's not for nothing that the idea of resilience became popular in the United States in the wake of the Vietnam War. A small army had defeated the world's greatest military and industrial power, and yet, for America, nothing had changed at all: not its dominant, not to say domineering position on the world stage, nor its overblown sense of national pride, nor its view of itself as custodian of the universal right to democratic freedom and the pursuit of happiness. More than a million Vietnamese and sixty thousand Americans had simply died in vain. In the years that followed, the US went on to cause further damage in Iraq and Afghanistan, again showing great resilience; that is, without the slightest dent to its self-esteem.

For Putin's Russia and Zelensky's Ukraine, resilience would mean returning, after the war, to what they were before – with an inescapable resumption of hostilities.

We should therefore be wary of resilience: in any difficult situation (not just wars), the obstacle to overcome is not the situation itself but the factors that caused it.

A bad relationship with the Overcoming Obstacles function can also be caused by not taking obstacles seriously enough and underestimating their difficulty. For President Johnson, in the sixties, this meant thinking, 'We'll destroy the Vietcong in a heartbeat.' For Putin, 'Ukraine will capitulate immediately.' For me and any other writer, 'I'll dash off this book in no time because I've already got all my ideas worked out.'

Failing to take things seriously prevents us from building up the skills we need not only to overcome but even to perceive the obstacles in front of us, thus depriving us of their positive effects: those skills are not accumulated, nor even produced. We remain as stupid as ever, which is the aim – conscious or otherwise – of many.

Again, the *stupiditas* here comes down to fear: a fear of the future, to be exact. Overcoming an obstacle necessarily takes us forward. 'Forward towards what?' a voice in our head always asks. 'If I move forward, I will change. I'll want more; what I have will no longer be enough; the people I mix with will no longer be enough for me. I'll have to justify myself to my friends; it will be uncomfortable, perhaps painful. I'll have to leave them behind. They'll feel betrayed. I'll know I've let them down. And I'll also be betraying myself: I won't be who I was before. True, if I don't overcome this obstacle, I'll be betraying the other "me" that overcoming this obstacle would have made me become. But that other me doesn't exist yet, and I do, the "me" as I am now. The other me can be aborted.'

This inner voice can become deafeningly loud.

QUESTION: 'How do you respond to this voice?'

ANSWER: 'You don't. If you keep moving, it disappears.'

ATTENTION

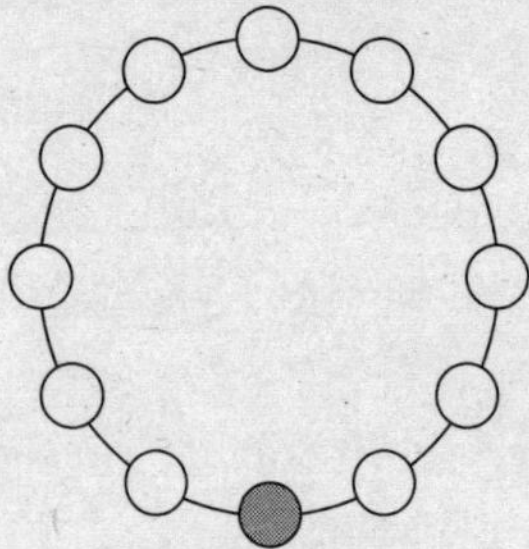

Do I notice?

Attention: from the Latin *tendere*, which meant not only 'to stretch', 'to tauten' or 'to hold out' but also 'to extend'.

Aestivam sermone benigno tendere noctem

These are the words of the poet Horace, inviting a friend to dinner a little over two thousand years ago: 'We will extend the summer night with friendly conversation.'

By paying attention, we stretch and extend our readiness to notice things. This is an act of will, which can be differentiated from simply sensing things (our senses sense many things we completely ignore) by using the verb 'to perceive', which means precisely: to notice having had certain sensations.

By paying attention, we also stretch and extend our world:

we stretch our inner world, and what we already know about the world;

we extend it towards something in the outside world which will either confirm or alter what we already know.

We are free to do both things exactly as we please, because our attention belongs to us and nobody else. And for the same reason, when a person makes use of their attention, they are, more than ever, at the centre of their own interior and exterior world. Like this:

1. You
2. Your interiority
3. The outside world

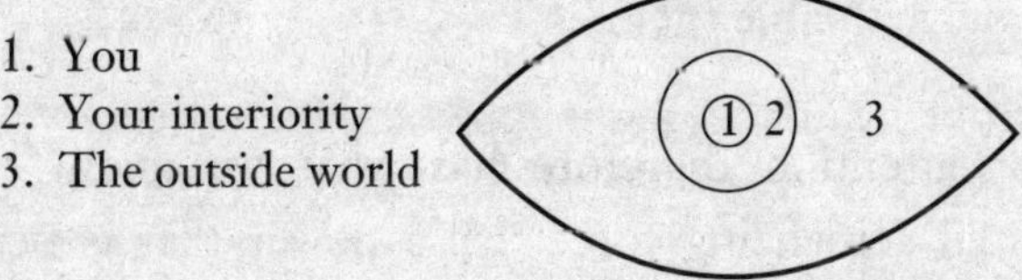

But that's not all. Your attention brings to life whatever you want, for just as long as you want, and no longer.

A certain star in the night sky;
a memory;
a goal;
a certainty;
God;
other gods;
the poet Horace and his dinner invitation;

Brontosauruses which died out millions of years ago;
the dolphins of the Tyrrhenian Sea;
a cat;
Bishop Berkeley's never disproved 1710 theory that existing simply means being perceived by someone, *esse est percipi*.

All of this exists, for you, only when you pay attention to it, and then it disappears. And nothing exists that doesn't exist for you.

QUESTION: 'That's not true; it can't be. There are loads of things that exist that I've never heard of, aren't there?'

ANSWER: 'Name them.'

Our attention therefore has what we might call an unlimited actualizing force. It's a power that is personal, absolute and inextinguishable: there is nothing anyone can do to undermine it. If I talk to you about something I have made exist for myself, it's up to you, and only you, to consider that thing and decide in what way and to what extent you want to make it exist for you, too. In other words, I can never truly control you, or only insofar as you allow me to (and vice versa). This can only be good news for those of us who believe in free will.

The bad news is the only things at your disposal are those made to exist for you. This is what Hamlet described: 'I could be bounded in a nutshell, and count myself a king of infinite space' (Act II, Scene II). You are king, director, lighting technician, playwright of everything – but 'everything', to you, is only your own version of everything, and it pales into insignificance when you compare it to what might have been, or might still be for you at any moment, *if only you were not bounded in a nutshell.*

The limit, the impenetrable nutshell of our attention lies in its inability to perceive itself: indeed, if it turned its focus on itself, it would stop being attention and become distraction. It's like the act of seeing: I can't observe my own pupils while they're looking around, because as soon as I try to do that, I stop looking around.

Is it possible for me to quantify the weaknesses in my Attention function by comparing my world (the size of the world that this function makes exist for me) with the size of someone else's?

No, because all I can ever know about someone else's world is what I make exist myself, inside my 'nutshell', and I see it the way I want it to be, regardless of what it's like for this other person.

For this reason, I believe Attention to be our authentic centre, the 'I', the psychic subject within us that says 'my life, my mind, my memories' and to which all the functions we have seen so far belong: the one which communicates in the Communication function, defends itself in the Self-Defence function, orients itself in external and internal space, knows or doesn't know itself to be wealthy and so on. And it is irreducible to anything else, incommunicable, undoubtedly movable, able to expand or contract its own world – *but is unknown to itself*: I cannot know my own self, because I am it. I am and always will be confined by the limits of my own knowledge, and will never know anything precise about this place I'm confined to.

The story of the word 'I' confirms this.

I

I, *io*, *ich*, *je*, *yo* and the Latin *ego* are all related to the Greek *egō*, which meant and still means 'I'. The etymology, and therefore the original meaning, of *egō* is still an enigma to many scholars.

Some (though not many) claim it has to do with the Greek word *éxis*, which signified various things: 'possession', 'condition' (the fact of possessing a lot or a little), 'temperament' (the moods one has), 'experience' (the memories one has), 'abilities' and 'body' (which are also possessions of sorts). It's not a bad hypothesis: *egō* would mean 'the one who possesses all of this'.

But *egō* is also related to the Greek particle *ex*, which means 'outside'. *Ex* derives from the Indo-European root *sek*, which meant 'to separate' (the word 'sex' derives from the same root). *Egō*, and *ego*, I, *io*, *ich*, *je* and *yo* could therefore refer to a state of alienation from everything, of being cut off from everything, even when you're right in the middle of it.

'I' is therefore a paradoxical *external centre* of everything – or of what 'everything' means to each of us. It is *ex* to such an extent that we are all in a condition of *stupiditas* with respect to it: we cannot understand it – just as philosophers have failed to define the concept of beauty or truth, and biologists cannot explain the origins of life, and Christians don't know God's name (the word 'God' is simply a job title).

Yet we rarely speak about this 'I' with due respect for its mysteries and its actualizing powers. When we say 'I' we actually mean something else, as we'll see in the next chapter.

QUESTION: 'So when I speak about myself, I'm not speaking about myself?'

ANSWER: 'No. You're only speaking about what you are lacking.'

QUESTION: 'Oh, really? Do psychologists know this?'

ANSWER: 'Not as far as I know.'

TWELVE VERSIONS OF 'I'

Just as the tongue always returns to the sore tooth, none of us can help using the pronoun 'I' both to say and, at the same time, to hide what's preventing us from developing one or more of our functions.

'I', in everyday parlance and also in our thoughts, is the name of a curse that throws us into a trap. In the best-case scenario, it becomes a cry for help: 'Set me free!' In the worst and most common case, we imagine this curse to be the theme of our lives, and consequently live badly.

Let's look at this in an orderly way.

Those with an underdeveloped Communication function give the name 'I' to a corridor leading to a closed door. It is a corridor filled with warped memories and set phrases designed to suit a number of conversation topics; the altogether more numerous topics on which these people have nothing to add are dismissed as too difficult or strange to bother with. Who or what is behind the door, they don't know.

When they say or think the phrase, 'I agree with this,' it means 'Here's something that means I won't have to open that door.'

Those with an underdeveloped Self-Defence function give the name 'I' to a mess of fears of the fear of fear, kept holed up in a bunker. More than anything, they fear the fear of the fear of who they really are.

When they say or think the phrase, 'I agree with this,' it means 'This doesn't scare me.'

Those with an underdeveloped External Direction function give the name 'I' to their reluctance to ask themselves questions about themselves: as soon as they do, they will begin to engage better with their surroundings, but they're always putting it off. Some of them are quite prepared to go on in this way forever, never asking themselves these questions, and meanwhile time ticks on.

The same goes for those with an underdeveloped Internal Direction function: these people also give the name 'I' to their own superficiality.

When they say or think the phrase, 'I agree with this,' it means 'This won't lead anyone to question me.'

Those with an underdeveloped Authority function give the name 'I' to their unconfessable eagerness to submit to someone, or their fake or exaggerated memories of failed or fruitless acts of rebellion.

When they say or think the phrase, 'I agree with this,' it means 'A lot of other people think this, too.'

Those with an underdeveloped Wealth function give the name 'I' to their reluctance (incomprehensible even to themselves) to value things they might love, if only they were brave enough.

When they say or think the phrase, 'I agree with this,' it means 'This won't cost me all that much.'

Those with an underdeveloped relationship with The Past function give the name 'I' to their own ignorance, but of course they don't know they're doing this: they're ignorant of their ignorance, and couldn't imagine how to begin to overcome it.

When they say or think the phrase, 'I agree with this,' it means 'This corresponds with what I already know.'

Those with an underdeveloped relationship with the Your Past function give the name 'I' to their inner adult, who occasionally tells twee little tales of their days of going or not going to nursery.

When they say or think the phrase, 'I agree with this,' it means 'This is a mature line of reasoning for a right-thinking person.'

Those with an underdeveloped Outsider function give the name 'I' to their own conformism.

When they say or think the phrase, 'I agree with this,' it means 'This won't get me into trouble.'

Those with an underdeveloped Sense of Obstacles function give the name 'I' to their own habits, their own reassuring predictability.

When they say or think the phrase, 'I agree with this,'

it means 'This is nothing new and so I'm not worried about it.'

Those with an underdeveloped Overcoming Obstacles function give the name 'I' to their own resignation.

When they say or think the phrase, 'I agree with this,' it means 'Well, there's nothing I can do about it, so let's just say it's fine as it is.'

Those who make poor use of their Attention function pronounce the pronoun 'I' more often than others. This doesn't mean their Attention is lacking (as we discussed earlier, this isn't possible, given that this function is always engaged in bringing the world to life, and its creations are always masterpieces) but that they are continually distracted, taking more notice of themselves than of anything else.

When they say or think the phrase, 'I agree with this,' it means 'I have decided to agree, although I'm not all that interested in the question, and therefore haven't really understood it.'

This is typical of people who are getting old, at any age.

None of these twelve forms of 'I' stupidity are irreparable: all you need do is recognize yourself in one or more of these scenarios, feel a bit silly about it, aim to do better and begin to change.

Here ends, for now, the practical section of the book. The many problems raised by the word 'I' and the concept of the self over the past 120 years, and psychologists' ludicrous claims to have understood and explained it, deserve further discussion and theoretical clarification, which I will set out in the next section. Readers uninterested in the history of science can happily skip this part and go straight to the Epilogue, which focuses on self-analysis, but in so doing will miss out on a few amusing stories and a couple of unusual lines of thinking.

QUESTION: 'Hang on, what do you mean by "getting old at any age"?'

ANSWER: 'An acquaintance of mine once told me, "Yes, I should have been a vet – it was always my true calling – but it's too late now, I'm already twenty-two."'

PART TWO

Theory

THE 'I' IN PSYCHOLOGY

Psychology studies our relationships with other people and ourselves, with realities and fantasies, with past and future, with social norms, with opportunities to change, to desire or not to desire . . . with everything.

It's a fascinating subject, the subject of all subjects: anything can be psychologized, since whatever we do, think or say implies and expresses our relationship to everything. For this reason, psychologists consider themselves more useful than experts in any other field of knowledge: they can painstakingly explain discoveries in physics, religious dogmas, art or geopolitics from a psychological perspective – whereas a physicist, theologian, artist or geopolitics expert would struggle to explain a psychological perspective without becoming a psychologist themselves.

Marlene Dietrich had her famous doubts, complaining that psychologists were trying to explain her films. Didn't they know a movie was just a movie? A psychologist would take this as evidence of denial, an attempt to hide something, a symptom. Until a few years ago, I would have done the same. But people do change their minds.

Psychology approaches its own vast subject matter in the belief that a relatively stable structure exists in all of us which governs our relationships with everything. At the beginning of the past century, this structure was named by Freud:

the ego

Meaning 'I' in Latin, the same structure is known as *l'Io* in Italian, *das Ich* in German, *le moi* in French, and so on. And the disciples of Freud, Jung and the other founders of modern psychology continue to use the same terminology. Only, it has never quite rung true.

I, *Ich*, *Io*, *Moi* are simply personal pronouns, colloquial terms for what, in order to satisfy the demands of scientific discourse, ought to be denoted by a *noun*. 'I' is the word our relationship-governing structure would use to talk about itself, and so calling that structure the ego, or 'the I', is like calling the *Felis catus* species 'the Meows' or the sub-species *Canis lupus familiaris* 'the Woofs', assuming that cats and dogs refer to themselves with the words 'meow' and 'woof' respectively. The ego, or 'the I', is a similarly cute and fun-sounding term, but we might have expected the science of psychology to come up with a more accurate taxonomy.

And the problem only becomes more complicated when we consider what psychology knows about this crucial structure of ours.

The first rule of any science is that it defines its scope, stating clearly what it is or isn't in the business of studying. An entomologist studies insects but not galaxies; an astronomer studies galaxies but not the Napoleonic wars. But how do we define the limits of the so-called 'ego'? When and how can we step outside these limits, so that we can be sure it is indeed the ego we are observing and not something else? All of us, even psychologists, have an ego, and we always will. We cannot perceive, seek, find, think, remember anything, except through our own ego. We can never step outside it, because if we did, we wouldn't perceive or know anything; we would be unconscious. Because of this, everything a psychologist analyses is in fact a form of self-analysis, a version of 'know thyself'. Which would be no bad thing, and actually very interesting for that psychologist, if only they were not a psychologist, that is, an exponent of a science which credulously claims it's possible to study the ego from outside.

If this were possible   if, that is, psychologists were somehow able to step outside their own ego and remain conscious, thus gaining the objectivity fundamental to every science – where would they go to look for someone else's ego?

Psychology seems to be satisfied with the belief that the ego is within the individual. What does this mean, exactly?

Within the body?

Not only there. From Freud onwards, psychologists have known that all of us project onto others a number of personal traits that, for one reason or another, make us uncomfortable: those who think too highly of themselves ascribe their own defects to other people, and those who think too poorly of themselves ascribe to someone else the desirable qualities they possess but daren't put to use. Thus, a part of the ego exists outside of us.

How big this part is, we don't know.

So looking for the ego within us won't get us very far.

To truly analyse a patient's ego, a psychologist would have to examine everyone on whom that patient had projected some aspect of themselves, including assorted politicians, actors, newspaper columnists, religious leaders, athletes and filmmakers this patient had never met in person, and who were, in many cases, dead. From studying these myriad other people, the psychologist could ascertain how much of them was simply a projection of the patient in question – a displaced, if possibly important, fragment of their personality – while taking great care not to project anything of themselves onto these same people. A monumental task that has never been undertaken and never will be.

If you want to study something, you must first locate it not only in space but also in time: I can't go and watch a game if I know where it's being played but not when. Perhaps psychologists believe they can study an ego on the basis of its current state, like a dentist examining a patient's molars. But you only have to look at a molar to establish what state it's currently in. To establish anything about a person's ego, you have to ask them for a certain amount of information.

This information consists for the most part of memories, half memories and false memories, and these memories change at every stage of our personal evolution or involution – even with every shift in mood. Much, then, of what we can find out about a person's ego is rooted in an uncertain past; even the most objective psychologist could still only analyse something that has mostly ceased to exist, with no documentary evidence – no X-rays, no blood counts, no CT scans – to support it.

It appears that, as far as psychology is concerned, the ego is more act of faith than true focus of study – just as the soul is in religion.

A priest who believes in the existence of the soul might become an investigator of souls – might, that is, have convinced himself that he is able to analyse souls, during confession, for example, just as psychoanalysts believe themselves to be engaged in the analysis of a patient's ego during a therapy session. There would be nothing wrong with this, if psychology were a religion – that is, if its goal were to soothe myriad worries with pleasing if unprovable affirmations.

But psychology is a science.

A science which rests on an act of faith might, as religions do, set out all manner of problems, but, as in religion, the only solutions it will be able to offer are ones which keep this act of faith intact. It won't be interested in the truth but in consistency with its own creed. It will devote its time to proving itself right – something true sciences never do.

Marlene Dietrich was correct. Psychology might claim to have something to say about everything, but when it comes down to it, it really only has anything to say about psychology. Meanwhile, a movie is a movie, and you are you, and psychology may have very little idea who you really are.

QUESTION: 'So I shouldn't bother going to see a shrink?'

ANSWER: 'Well, assuming they're a nice enough person, I don't see why not. It'll be an experience, after all.'

THE CASE OF JUNG

Carl Gustav Jung, a disciple and later opponent of Freud, had serious doubts about what psychology was able to say about the ego, and *almost* managed to grasp the implications of this. It's this *almost* that makes him an interesting and ethically complex case, worthy of greater understanding.

In his 1921 book *Psychological Types*, Jung set out the idea that the ego has four key 'functions' at its disposal: thinking, feeling, sensation and intuition. Each of these functions is, according to Jung, a way of exploring the world:

we use thinking when we ask ourselves why something is as it is;
we use feeling when we are interested in how a thing or person pleases or disappoints us;
we use sensation when we are observing the details of any given thing;
we use intuition when we ask ourselves what's hiding behind a situation or how we might improve it.

These four functions are complementary: in order to ask yourself why something is as it is (thinking), it's useful to observe it in detail (sensation); the pleasant or unpleasant impressions produced by a certain thing (feeling) are also derived from observation (sensation) and, along with thinking, are useful if you want to discover hidden sides to that thing, or to perfect it (intuition).

But, says Jung, it's rare for anyone to make use of all four functions at once: usually, one of them gains the upper hand in infancy, becomes the superior function and remains so for life. Another function is neglected, declines and becomes the inferior function for life; the two remaining functions develop only partially, one slightly more than the other, without ever rivalling the superior function, and Jung calls these the auxiliary functions.

While describing the overall dynamic of the functions, Jung must have had something like the circular diagram below in mind, similar to the mandalas he liked to draw (he was fond of Indian mysticism):

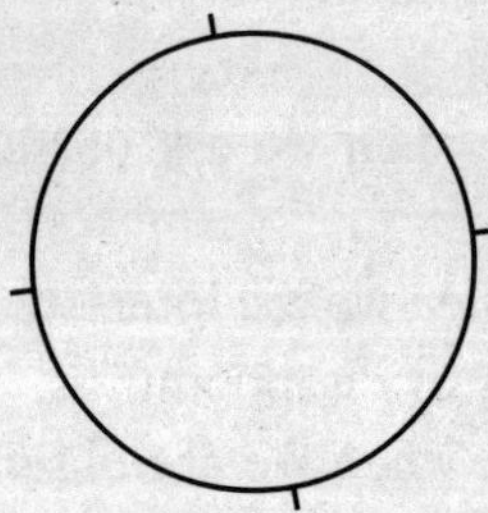

The superior function at the top, the inferior function at the bottom, and the two auxiliary functions halfway up the circumference – one slightly higher than the other.

As well as a mandala, Jung must have been thinking of a compass. According to his theory, each function is diametrically opposed to another, as north is to south and east is to west. Thinking is opposed to feeling, and sensation to intuition. Indeed, it's self-evident that the values and priorities of thinking and feeling are polar opposites, and that sensation – that is, attention to things as they are – is different from intuition, which imagines how things might be.

The four Jungian functions are not only complementary – and this is the key, and most compelling point – they are also *competitive*: each function understands and decides things in its own way, but it does so just as well as any other. So a person who has an over-developed feeling function can be just as intelligent, cultured, dynamic and likeable as someone with an over-developed thinking, intuition or sensation function. They all share the same level of understanding of the world, they just have different qualities and ways of going about things.

Jung built on all of this – in particular, the fact that the dominant function remained so for life – to set out a universal typology dividing people into four basic 'psychological types' on the basis of their dominant function.

The Thinking Type, for example, would be illustrated like this:

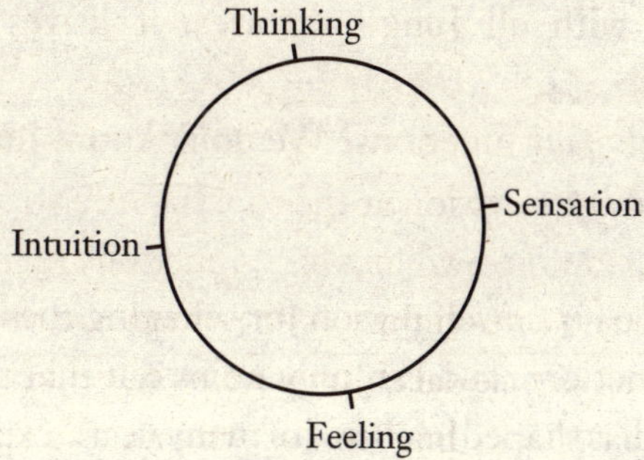

These are individuals who are good at thinking, but not so well equipped for dealing with matters of feeling.

The Sensation Type (with sensation at the top of the circle and intuition at the bottom) has a good eye and healthy appetites but shouldn't rely on their own intuition, which will invariably lead them astray.

The Feeling Type struggles to make decisive arguments.

The Intuition Type complicates their own basic needs – for food, sleep, physical activity, sex.

Thus, according to Jung, everyone, even a genius, is stupid in some respect.

Jung gave detailed descriptions of each of these four basic types, listing their peculiar behaviours, the different ways in which they were extroverted or introverted, the careers to which they were best suited and the afflictions and difficulties they were most likely to suffer, as well as advising how they might choose a partner. He gave examples of his four types in the famous artists, theologians, saints, philosophers and other notable figures of the past.

Jung's typology has the great benefit of being simple, straightforward and immediately applicable.

But, as with all Jung's theories, it leaves too much unexplained.

Why only *four* functions? We don't know. Jung wrote in *Psychological Types*:

I can give no *a priori* reason for selecting these four as basic functions, and can only point out that this conception has shaped itself out of many years' experience.

Could the 'many years' experience' of a single psychiatrist working solely in Zurich really prove that, across the ages and continents, there had only ever been four basic functions, and that the dominant function remained the same for life? No, but Jung seems to have brushed this aside.

It's a strange thing for a scientist to devise a universal typology with such apparent haste.

Jung, in 1921, seemed so excited by his theory that he was bursting to share it, and yet he couldn't quite get his words out. A *stupiditas* was holding him back. We can see it in the questions the Jungian theory of types raises and leaves unanswered.

First of all, what is the relationship between the four functions and the ego? Are the functions at the service of the ego, as the angels are to God (the inferior function being the Devil), or is the ego contained entirely within its functions, *and nowhere else*?

This second possibility is not confirmed by Jung, but it is implied by his use of the word *type*: a type defines what we are, to the exclusion of all else.

It's different from being, let's say, a doctor or a refuse collector: our profession doesn't tell us who we are, only what we do for certain hours of the day.

It's different from being tense, calm, lazy or inquisitive, or anything else you might be at some times and not others. According to Jung, an Intuition Type (like me) is not and will never be one of the other types. So the ego doesn't possess or use its own functions, nor is it mastered by them: it *is* them.

*

No matter – a diehard Jungian might say – all this means is that studying the ego is like studying an operating system, in the same way that studying a computer means studying its internal mechanisms, even if that computer is capable of reasoning, speaking and writing.

No. The mechanisms of a computer perform a number of specific tasks, like the organs of our body: the hard disk isn't the same as the screen, and the mouse isn't the same as the plug, just as the stomach isn't responsible for breathing and the eyes aren't responsible for touch. The four Jungian functions, on the other hand, compete to do the same thing: as we saw above, each of them represents a way of behaving and exploring the world. They are four minds, four consciousnesses, four memories, *four different 'me's*. And we are two of them in particular: the dominant 'me'-function, which steers us, and the inferior function, which is our stupidity and holds us back. But at birth we were all four of them, says Jung, and with a bit of luck and a lot of work, who knows? Perhaps we might become them again.

So we're all made up of four parts? If we're all fourfold, each of us is not one alone, and thus the ego psychology talks about doesn't exist. I (ego) is a singular pronoun; the plural is *we*. Are you a 'we', even if a single reflection greets you in the mirror?

Jung, as I said, doesn't dare to draw this conclusion.

And yet he must have read *Strange Case of Dr Jekyll and Mr Hyde*. Jung was interested in the supernatural from a young age, and he would have been fourteen in 1889 when the bestselling Gothic horror was translated into German.

In the last chapter of the book, Dr Jekyll, a scientist fascinated by mysticism, writes in his diary:

I thus drew steadily nearer to that truth, by whose partial discovery I have been doomed to such a dreadful shipwreck: that man is not truly one, but truly two. I say two, because the state of my own knowledge does not pass beyond that point. Others will follow, others will outstrip me on the same lines; and I hazard the guess that man will be ultimately known for a mere polity of multifarious, incongruous and independent denizens.

Proceeding in a similar vein, Jung was close to arriving at four incongruous subjects. Did he fear a Jekyllian shipwreck? During the 1920s, people were still talking about the outlandish ideas of Rudolf Steiner and Nietzsche – the former judged too eccentric, the latter having sunk into madness. Did Jung fear being associated with these two, threatening his position as an esteemed scientist? Was his hesitancy therefore *stupiditas* caused by deficiencies in the Self-Defence and Outsider functions?

It's a possibility. In his autobiography *Memories, Dreams, Reflections* (which, in accordance with his wishes, was published only after his death in 1961) he describes, as early as the 1910s, having often encountered spiritual guides in his garden. One of these invisible teachers gave him lessons in psychology: he told Jung it was naive to believe that we generate our thoughts; rather, it was wiser to view one's thoughts as animals in a forest, people in a room, or birds in flight. And Jung, in admiration, admitted he had drawn insights from this into what he called psychic objectivity.

Jung attributes to a spiritual guide the notion that an individual's psyche is a crowded room, or a forest filled with life, with flocks of birds flying between the trees: the hypothesis of a *plural* dimension. In every era, we find examples of people attributing to creatures of dream or fantasy, angels or demons, what they dared not admit having thought for themselves. And in his account of these conversations, Jung reserves himself the role of stupid disciple slowly progressing towards enlightenment.

Not that he progressed all that much: after 1921, Jung continued to refer to the ego in the singular. Publicly casting doubt on the issue would have meant destroying the foundations of modern psychology, which Jung himself had built alongside Freud: here, too, he feared a 'shipwreck'. Sadly, great scientists and philosophers who go to great efforts to build a system rarely abandon that system to build another from scratch. It's *stupiditas* caused by weaknesses in the Authority and Sense of Obstacles functions.

> QUESTION: 'How can I find out which psychological type I'm supposed to be?'
>
> ANSWER: 'You can find various questionnaires by searching online for "Jung type test". Or, if you have time, have a look at the last 180 or so pages of Jung's *Psychological Types*.'

WHAT IF

History isn't to be written in what-ifs, according to some. But I don't see why not. In the history of science, in particular, the subordinating conjunction 'if' can be extremely useful.

What would have happened if Jung, following on from Jekyll's epiphany, had set out the theory that each of us has not one but several egos, several versions of I or me? The psychological dogma of the single ego would have come to be seen as an initial, ultimately mistaken hypothesis based on the assumption that since we have only one body, we must have only one ego.

Ideas of internal conflict and harmony would have been developed in new ways. New problems and perspectives would have been uncovered. For example, what if:

Each of our various 'me's is able to work together or against one another, at different times?

I become unhappy when one of my 'me's ignores what another or several other 'me's of mine are saying?

Those who seek the truth know the thrill of finding it, and perhaps discover truths great and small when all their 'me's are aligned, and if we never seem to achieve this, it's only because we are marginalizing one or more of our 'me's?

The voices we seem to hear in our heads when we're tired are distorted perceptions of the 'me's we normally condemn to silence?

The Christian trinity represents the partial discovery of our internal plurality?

The Devil is a millennial symbol for an excluded 'me'?

The twelve apostles were all Jesus?

Abide in me as I in you [. . .] I am the vine and you the branches

What if this passage from the Gospels (John 15:4–5) is a foretaste of Jung, and thus of Dr Jekyll before him, and we have completely misunderstood the Gospel?

These are just a handful of the many, many questions that might have opened new horizons for psychology in 1921, had Jung heeded the advice of his spiritual guide. Thankfully, in science, no question that emerges from a 'what if' is wasted.

QUESTION: 'Wait a minute – aren't you going to answer all those questions?'

ANSWER: 'Do I need to? Take away the "what if" and the question marks and they've answered themselves.'

THE BIG FIVE

The theory of psychological types is the most popular of Jung's theories today, and not only because it's his simplest.

A scientific or philosophical theory gains popularity either because it explains a great deal (like the theory of relativity) or because it promises a great deal (like quantum mechanics). Jungian typology belongs to the second category. Whether or not it's clear what this second kind of theory promises is largely beside the point. The most powerful promises are those which allow us to imagine as yet unnamed and unimagined futures; paradoxically, a theory may be better able to speak to us when it leaves some things unsaid, inviting those who come after it to fill in the blanks – though whether later generations do indeed go further is by no means guaranteed.

Thus, from the 1950s onwards, and especially since the 1980s, psychologists in the USA have produced ever more typologies, some of which draw upon the Jungian framework: circular diagrams whose components are called traits, or facets, or factors, or dimensions, partly to distinguish themselves from Jung. What these typologies describe is not the ego (the term having by now largely fallen out of favour) but instead the so-called *personality*.

Another unfortunate choice of word: 'personality' derives from *persona*, meaning 'mask' in Latin. *Personae* were the masks actors wore on stage. 'Personality' would therefore indicate what an individual decides to show to others, rather than the largely secret interior structure that has always been the main focus of psychology.

But in drawing up their diagrams, American, or American-style, psychologists have overlooked this terminological error – a (Freudian) slip which ought to have piqued their professional interest.

Some of these personality diagrams are needlessly complex; none are exhaustive. I'm including only the best-known one below, which instead of four functions has five traits and thus entered the history of psychology as the 'Big Five':

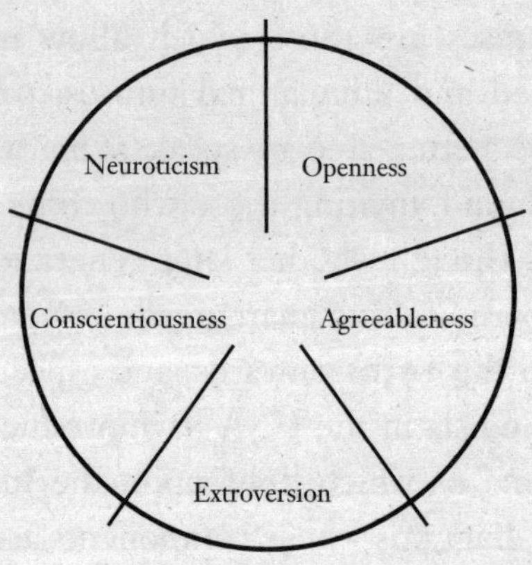

It's also referred to as the OCEAN model, an acronym for the five traits:

Openness, meaning receptiveness to stimuli and new ideas;

Conscientiousness, meaning self-discipline, determination, the ability to approach things practically and systematically;

Extroversion, meaning sociability, empathy and vivaciousness;

Agreeableness, meaning the ability to please others, which includes honesty, trustworthiness, tolerance, kindness and modesty;

Neuroticism, meaning tendency for neurotic behaviour, such as anxiety, catastrophizing, bitterness or impulsiveness.

You must use these exact five words in all scientific discussions of people, insist the countless proponents of the Big Five theory, because in all the dictionaries in the world there is no vocabulary better suited to describing personality, and because only these five traits are universal, and can thus be evaluated in all human beings without exception.

Both of these arguments are well supported: American psychologists really did spend a long time searching through dictionaries and carried out large numbers of individual tests to measure the Big Five across every continent.

And yet it is possible to find weaknesses in both arguments:

a science doesn't depend on dictionaries but creates its own terminology, if it knows what it's talking about and wants to talk about it;

it's obvious that character traits denoted by commonly used words are very widespread, but obvious things add nothing to science.

In spite of this, the Big Five still represents the most widely respected schema for mapping personality – psychology's replacement for the ego. The relationship between personality and the five traits has, of course, been examined, the conclusion being that the five traits make up an individual's personality, just as our features make up our face. This is important: in making this decision, American psychologists ruled out the possibility that you or I consist of anything other than the way we react, experience happiness or sadness, approach our commitments and respond to other people. Personality (the ex-ego) is all there is to know about any of us, and it is, to use the technical term, an *emergent property* of the five traits. Of course, everyone has their own personality, because the five traits vary from person to person; the Big Five model allows these variations to be easily classified and carefully studied.

The criticisms levelled against the Big Five theory over the past forty years have not succeeded in undermining its popularity. Which is odd, because it's a shoddy theory for at least three reasons:

First, the Big Five are qualities which pertain to social relations. It's when we are with other people, and especially when we are working with others, that the extent to which we are mentally open, sociable, courteous, conscientious or neurotic becomes obvious. The Big Five model – unlike the

Jungian typology – tells us nothing about what we perceive or understand about reality or unreality, or the value we give to what we know or don't know, or the way we treat ourselves, or what makes us smile or cry when nobody's looking. And yet we do still exist, even when no one else can see us.

Second, the Big Five theory is useful in recruitment. There's a reason why a version of the model was first used to rate officer candidates at a Texan Air Force base in 1957 (at that point, the five traits were referred to as: *Surgency*, which is almost synonymous with extroversion; *Dependability*; *Agreeableness*, which the next generation of psychologists also liked; *Emotional Stability*, which sounds better than neuroticism; and *Culture*, which would come to be replaced by *Openness*, perhaps because 'culture' sounded too highfalutin). The model is used to establish to what extent an individual can serve a form of authority. And yet we don't exist purely to serve others.

Third, the Big Five theory is designed to set our minds at rest. It makes us believe that whatever adjustment problems we may have can be resolved by improving our Big Five: taking tranquillizers to reduce our neuroticism and upping our levels of extroversion, agreeableness, conscientiousness and openness. If a personality theory sets out to appease us, it's not a theory but a form of brainwashing.

The reason the Big Five model has been so successful in America is because of its very Americanness. The reasons it's taken seriously in other parts of the world are, firstly, compulsive veneration for all things American, and, secondly, the fact that it explains personality (the ego, as was) as an emergent property – as the product, rather than the cause, of psychic activity.

The cult of the American is just a habit.

The idea that personality is only an emergent property, on the other hand, represents a huge shift. It's a big step forward from what Jung couldn't quite bring himself to say. What it means is that at the centre, at the origin of psychic activity, there's nothing. We are nothing but the series of effects we produce, and none of these effects links back to anything else. The ego was a naive illusion. Still less credible is the idea that your personality came into being at the moment of your birth: your Big Five were formed later, and your personality was formed from them; and it will last as long as your Big Five last, after which comes nothing.

The whole story of you is here. The rest is silence.

QUESTION: 'Why do I get the feeling this isn't actually the whole story of me?'

ANSWER: 'I've asked myself the same question.'

QUESTION: 'Who's the *stupidus*, then? You and me, or those psychologists?'

ANSWER: 'Let's find out.'

WHY THERE'S MORE TO IT THAN THAT

Let's recap.

Freud said: we all have an ego, just one per person. And the Freudians went along with this.

Jung almost managed to say: no, we all have a number of different egos, let's say four. And the Jungians took no notice.

American psychologists say: 'ego' is an inadequate term; the true subject within us is a collection of psychological traits we call personality.

How do we know who's right?

We can't.

In psychology, no one can objectively demonstrate their theory is correct. It's a point we've already gone over (on page 101): psychologists' work is a matter of 'know thyself', and each of them is – like anyone else – the world authority on their own interior life.

Freud was under the impression he had a single ego.

Jung believed he had four.

Personality researchers imagine themselves to have and to be a mere assortment of character and behavioural traits.

I, who am not a psychologist, like my idea of twelve

functions, one of which strongly resembles what psychologists named the ego.

Neither I nor any psychologist can be sure that the conclusions we draw from introspection apply equally to other people. Anyone building a psychological theory can only *hope* that others, in their own efforts to get to know themselves, might reach the same conclusions as we have. In psychology, unlike any other science, the value of a theory depends above all on its emotional powers of persuasion; statistical evidence, tests and laboratory experiments count for little. Freud never devised a test to prove the Oedipus complex, and yet his theory held sway in the popular imagination for more than a century.

Because of this, we should consider psychology less a science than a branch of literature. A novel wins us over when it provides an insight into ourselves, and others, and everything around us, shedding new light on things we have seen but failed to notice. Psychological theories work in exactly the same way: they have to tell the whole story, and tell it well, or they're a disappointment.

There's an important element missing from the theory-fictions of Freud, Jung and the psychologists of personality, and from my own theory of twelve functions, and that's the protagonist.

Supposing, as Freud did, I have a single ego. I can feel I have it, but who is it, in me, that feels this?

I can feel, as Jung did, my four egos, but again: whoever it is, in me, that has those egos, is none of those four. Who is it, then? The same goes for my twelve functions.

And I can feel, as the psychologists of personality do,

that I am contained entirely in my personality, which is to say, in my reputation. But who, in me, feels this?

Until we can answer this question, our psychological story remains unfinished.

QUESTION: 'And if we find the answer, then what does it mean for me?'

ANSWER: 'You'll have more problems with the pronoun "I".'

QUESTION: 'Haven't we had enough problems?'

ANSWER: 'No, thank goodness.'

THE SELF

Freud established the ego as the highest point of the psyche. Above it there were only ideals and norms constructed by the ego itself (the so-called superego); below it, the deep, nasty, crude, grotesque unconscious. This narrative arc satisfied Freud. But not Jung. Jung was troubled not only by the questions:

Who does my ego belong to?
Who expresses themselves through my ego?

... but also by the fact that for thousands of years, humans had imagined, believed in and above all *felt* the existence of a higher power. This 'something more' had to be written into the story of psychology: human beings would never have come up with the idea of a god if the ego was truly the pinnacle of everything. Every religion had acted on this feeling, so why hadn't psychology?

'Because psychology isn't a religion,' Freud might have cut in. 'Religions are ancient and we're all about progress.'

Not to be dissuaded, Jung went on to use theological arguments to devise a psychological, rather than religious, image of what this thing beyond the ego might be, taking inspiration from the way in which certain Christian luminaries had devised God.

According to a medieval argument for God's existence, God is the greatest of all things, greater than all our wildest imaginings, because if this weren't so, we would be able to imagine something even greater, and we cannot. And Jung believed this thing beyond the ego was truly *great*.

In the seventeenth century, Descartes offered another proof of the existence of God: God is the height of all perfection, so he must exist, because he wouldn't be quite so perfect if he lacked existence. Jung came to believe that this thing greater than the ego must be the *totality* of a person's psychic phenomena; in other words, everything we might be, want, feel, understand or create if we were not limited to the little we are aware of being.

In this way, Jung also found the psychological solution to a wonderful enigma of Saint Paul (Jung's father was a Protestant pastor):

'When that which is perfect comes, then that which
is only in part shall be expunged [. . .] Now we see
as in a mirror, and all is an enigma; then we will
see face to face. Now I know in part, but then I will
know as I am known.'

1 Corinthians 13:12

We will keep growing until we meet God, Paul tells us, and then not only will we know everything, but we will know how we know it.

In the same way, reasoned Jung, this psychic totality

knows what we are yet to discover about ourselves. And, just like God, it sometimes reveals itself to us through visions, dreams, myths and legends. Because of our own limitations, this totality is, like God, for the time being 'irrepresentable', as Jung wrote in the last chapter of *Psychological Types*. Nevertheless, psychology's story at last had an ending; a scientific equivalent had been found for the 'something more' that only religions had previously dared mention, and we could now begin to study it in more detail.

Empirical evidence of this hypothesis: none.

Statistical data: none.

Emotional persuasiveness factor: high.

Jung gave this 'something more' a name: the Self (*das Selbst*). Here, too, he drew on metaphysics: 'Self' is the usual translation of the Sanskrit word *ātman*, which in Hinduism and Buddhism refers to the unfathomable, ineffable essence of an individual – what Western religions call the soul.

QUESTION: 'And that's not right?'

ANSWER: 'No.'

QUESTION: 'Why not just stick with this idea of Jung's? If there's no way of proving it, you just have to believe in it; it feels good to believe in something.'

ANSWER: 'Disbelieving feels even better.'

THE SELF?

But once again, Jung couldn't quite commit.

In the last chapter of *Psychological Types*, he argued that the Self is, strictly speaking, 'a postulate' and, on the next page, that the Self is 'only a working hypothesis'. Jung must have understood the meaning of these two scientific terms, and so this represents a slip of the pen, since a postulate that is only a hypothesis is not a postulate at all. Indeed:

> a postulate is a principle we assume to be true, in order to help us explain certain things or frame a problem (for example, 'through any point not on a given line, there exists exactly one line parallel to the given line' is one of Euclid's postulates);
> a hypothesis, on the other hand, is of no use at all unless proven correct.

We commit slips of this kind when we are trying to hide something from ourselves. What Jung was hiding here was the suspicion that the Self was only a provisional, improvable hypothesis, hastily mistaken for a postulate.

His suspicions were well founded. Jung's concept of the

Self, as with so much of his work, left too many questions unanswered:

> If the Self is 'irrepresentable', how can it be studied? That is, how can we be sure that what we glimpse in visions, dreams and myths is actually the Self?
> Above all, how do we know we should talk about the Self *in the singular*? Couldn't it be plural, like the angels, or the gods of polytheistic religions?

And if the Self is a totality superior to the ego, why call it the Self? 'Self' is a suffix used to form reflexive pronouns. It denotes the result of the mental operation a person performs when they reflect on their knowledge of themselves: in grammatical terms, then, 'myself' is less than 'I', since what you know about yourself is less than what you are.

'Self' is not even an accurate translation for *ātman*: *ātman*, in Sanskrit, means what we truly are, beyond appearances, and even beyond space and time; if a Western equivalent exists, it might, as I previously suggested, be 'soul'.

One last thing. In his forays into Indian mysticism, why did Jung stop at *ātman*? There was plenty more to find, if only he had dug a little deeper.

QUESTION: 'Like what?'

ANSWER: 'Nothingness.'

ANĀTMAN

An- in Sanskrit is a prefix meaning 'non', and some Buddhist traditions teach that the *ātman* doesn't exist, that we don't actually have a fundamental essence: instead, beneath all the characteristics we claim for ourselves, beneath everything we ever believed ourselves to be, there is only an *anātman* – not an essence, but an absence. It's akin to saying we don't have a soul, if by soul we mean a permanent identity. Or in psychological terms, it's akin to saying that beyond the experiences of our conscious ego and our memory of these experiences, there is nothingness.

What's striking about these 'soulless' branches of Buddhism is that they are anything but materialistic; on the contrary, they are about as spiritual as it gets. In Hinduism, from which Buddhism was born and later distanced itself, gaining knowledge of one's own *ātman* is the great mystical endeavour, representing freedom from illusion, torment, desire and expectation. But in the eyes of those who teach *anātman*, this vast spiritual exercise does not go far enough. The work of meditation, prayer and sacrifice is undoubtedly important but represents only the first step towards understanding that the *ātman* is merely an artifice, a narrative device used to give a false sense of continuity to the account we give others and ourselves of the various incidents of our lives.

So if we ask ourselves, 'Am I really the same person who used to crawl around the house on my hands and knees? And who got a D in maths? And who gave that fumbling first kiss? And who quit a year after getting their first pay cheque?' a Hindu might respond, 'You weren't the same person then as you are today. You've changed many times, been many people; the one who has always been inside you is your *ātman*.' The Hindu would feel satisfied with the response he or she had given, just like a Jew, Christian or Muslim, who would have said instead, 'It was your soul.' Teachers of *anātman*, on the other hand, would invite you to see this explanation as both too easy and at the same time too complicated. You have to cut out the 'who'. Your life has only been a series of 'whats'. Are you brave enough to do it? It's not easy. Simplicity never is.

Members of other Buddhist traditions and Hindus (among whom I count some of my dearest friends) argue that the doctrine of *anātman* is simply a meditation exercise, helpful for learning the attitude of detachment character-istic of the enlightened: a case of 'Imagine if you weren't really anything, and see what effect it has on you.' But for more than two thousand years, the teachers of *anātman* have been saying otherwise: it's not an 'Imagine if' but a 'Realize your own nothingness, when you're capable of doing so.'

Knowing thyself, therefore, means knowing a person of our own invention. Nothingness, after all, can never be known.

QUESTION: 'But am I my own nothingness, or am I me?'

ANSWER: 'Before nothingness, you're your various "me"s; beyond your "me"s, you're your nothingness.'

QUESTION: 'And beyond the nothingness?'

ANSWER: 'There's only a before nothingness.'

QUESTION: 'Why do I feel like I don't get it? Is this a *stupiditas*?'

ANSWER: 'Yes. It's the ultimate *stupiditas*, and reaching it is a beautiful thing.'

A NOTE ON NOTHINGNESS

Clarifying your thoughts on nothingness doesn't require you to add anything to what you already know. It only requires you to take away what you already know.

This kind of subtraction is something we're all rather good at. For example, we find the pronoun 'me' like this:

humanity minus other people = me.

The adverb 'now' is:

time minus the past and the future = now.

My soul is:

me minus my body = my soul.

And nothingness is:

Everything minus everything = nothingness.

But this is only the first part of the problem. Can I say that nothingness exists? If I say that nothingness exists, it is not nothingness, because nothingness cannot exist: nothingness can do nothing. But if I say that nothingness doesn't exist, that means that everything is everything everywhere, and nothingness is impossible – in which case how could we understand the meaning of the word 'nothingness' or how it ever occurred to anyone?

A logical solution to this would be: it's impossible to say anything about nothingness because whatever you say is something, and a nothing cannot be defined by a something. This would make it pointless to try to talk about nothingness. It's reminiscent of the difficulty Saint Augustine evokes of any attempt to talk about God:

si comprehendis non est Deus.

If you've understood what it is, it is not God.

We can only describe nothingness and God by saying what they are not. All that there is looks upon these and is still.

QUESTION: 'Why is our "me" surrounded by these indescribable things?'

ANSWER: 'If they weren't indescribable, we wouldn't be surrounded by them.'

REIFICATION

So all we know for certain about nothingness is that we don't know. And that's as it should be.

This negative knowledge can help guide our self-exploration, if beyond the 'me' inside us, our nothingness begins. And if it does, it's good news for all of us: it means that whatever we have to say about the psyche, there will always be more to say; that no psychologist will ever be able to say to a patient, or to themselves, 'There you go, we've understood everything about you and there's nothing else to know.' Our inner nothingness, our *anātman*, could help us resist definition: beyond what it's possible to know about ourselves, we would be like beauty, goodness or truth – concepts philosophy has failed to define. We would be like Augustine's God, since we could say:

si comprehendis non est me.

'If you've understood it, it isn't me.'

This would mark a step forward for psychologists, too. They could throw off the naive, pseudoscientific and para-religious pretense of having explained everything, and only then would their science become a way towards a truth it can never reach, like theoretical physics, but instead of studying universes, studying what we are.

We can, after all, *feel* this indescribable quality about us. It's what we have in mind when we talk about the soul in romantic terms: describing someone as your soul-mate means lending them this indescribable quality, this immensity.

> IMMENSITY: from the Latin *immensus*,
> formed from the prefix *in-*, meaning 'non',
> and the verb *metiri*, 'to measure'. Something
> is immense when it cannot be measured.

We know, or rather we feel we know, what immensity is, even if nothing is truly immeasurable except nothingness. How could we possibly know this, if not from ourselves? We know it because we *are* it, even if psychology is yet to grasp this. And it's this immensity within us that says 'me', 'my ego', 'myself', or 'I'.

When, as educated people, we talk about the soul, we're referring to something else entirely, giving the word the meanings decreed by our religions – all of which impose limitations on this immensity. Indeed, the soul, in religious contexts, is a reification.

> TO REIFY: To make 'a thing' out of something
> that isn't a thing (a *res*, in Latin). For example,
> people can be reified, when they're considered
> only as manpower; romantic relationships, when

they're commodified; artworks, when thought of as purely commercial products, and so on.

Yet even the limitations our religions impose on the soul can be of use to us, because they are as systematic as they are contradictory: they ring out clearly but don't ring true, attempting to reduce the irreducible; we can choose to believe in them, as so many do, or we can try to unpack them, and find enjoyment in doing so.

In the coming chapters we'll look first at some ancient insights into our intrinsic nothingness, then at some of the contradictions that make the soul as described by religion a metaphysical *stupiditas*.

QUESTION: 'Systematic reification? Do you mean religions have done this on purpose?'

ANSWER: 'When it comes to religion, everything is done on purpose.'

LIGHTNESS

Not only in India but in other ancient civilizations, the idea of an inner nothingness was a popular one.

In the Egyptian myth of psychostasy, or 'soul-weighing', the god Anubis was said to place a person's *ka* on one side of the scales and a feather on the other. The *ka* is an Egyptian equivalent of what we call the soul; the feather symbolizes Maat, the goddess of truth. If the *ka* was found to be heavier than the feather, the person would be devoured by Ammit, a goddess who was part crocodile, part lion and part hippo. Otherwise, the person would be declared *maa-kheru*, meaning 'just', 'justified' or 'in line with the truth'.

Egyptologists have always been confident that psychostasy happened after death, in the afterlife (*Duat*, in Egyptian), and thus that the Egyptian conception of the soul – along with a form of Last Judgement and Hell – was more or less aligned with ours. But here, as so often, Egyptologists have projected their own beliefs onto the Egyptians, in the mistaken assumption that their own views and values were valid across the ages. If proof were needed, we need only look at the fact that the most famous papyrus explaining psychostasy was named the *Book of the Dead* by

Egyptologists, when the original Egyptian title was *Spells for Going Forth by Day*.

I am of the mind that *Duat*, as the Egyptians saw it, was not so much an afterlife as an Elsewhere, a parallel dimension to *every moment of our lives*. Psychostasy didn't only happen after death, it was happening all the time, and anyone whose *ka* was heavier than a feather – only slightly heavier than nothing – was liable to be devoured by Ammit at any moment. This corresponds with the doctrine of *anātman*, according to which anyone who gives weight to their own *ātman* will be burdened with endless suffering (*dukkha* in Sanskrit).

The handing over of the *ka* to be weighed by Anubis, as described in *Spells for Going Forth by Day*, is a moment of wonder: what it shows is that the *ka* is merely an object, and one we can do without. Happiness comes when this object proves to be empty; it's what we continue to describe as 'taking a weight off our chests'.

QUESTION: 'What type of stupidity are these Egyptologists committing?'

ANSWER: 'It's a weakness in their relationship with The Past.'

HATING THE SOUL

In the Gospel according to Luke (14:26), Jesus refuses to accept as his disciple anyone who doesn't hate 'his own *psykhē*'. Most versions of the Bible translate the word *psykhē* as 'life', leading us to believe that Jesus was encouraging his disciples to hate the lifestyle they had followed up until that point. But in Greek (the language in which the Gospels were written) the word *psykhē* had four meanings, none of which is reducible to 'lifestyle':

vital principle;
character;
way of thinking;
ghost.

These four senses of the word were not distinct and separate from one another: it was believed that a person's individual life force was so fully expressed through their character and way of thinking that there was no way of drawing a line between any of these elements, and that this vital principle-character-way of thinking was what remained of a person after their death. *Psykhē* is therefore the equivalent of 'soul', and the Romans rightly translated the passage as:

Si quis venit ad me et non odit [. . .] animam suam, non potest meus esse discipulus.

'If someone comes to me and does not hate [. . .] his soul, he cannot be my disciple.'

A devout Christian would not imagine it possible for someone to be so thoroughly sick of their soul as to hate it, nor for Jesus ever to ask such a thing; it's one of the reasons many devout Christians don't read the Gospels very closely. The evangelists, on the other hand, must have known or have discovered that the *psykhē* was, like an illusion or a source of annoyance, something we were better off without. Elsewhere they write:

Whoever wants to save his psykhē will lose it.
Luke 9:24, Mark 8:35, Matthew 16:25, John 12:25

All four Gospels are in agreement here: it must have been a key point for the early Christians.

QUESTION: 'These passages from the Gospels really change the way we look at things. How can this be?'

ANSWER: 'Lots of passages from the Gospels change the way we look at things. Remember what we were saying about Aladdin's lamp, back on page 60?'

PAUL AND FRANCIS

Saint Paul writes, around 56 AD:

> Feel in yourselves what Jesus felt in himself: He
> was a form of God, and thus saw no abuse in being
> equal to God, but emptied himself, took the form
> of a servant, became similar to men, appeared like
> a man.
>
> Philippians 2:5–7

Paul of Tarsus often gives the impression of saying slightly more than he meant to. Here he states that Jesus was God and made himself man, and in order to do so, he emptied himself of everything he was. So far, so uncontroversial: more and more people at the time believed this to be what had happened. But Paul also says: Jesus did it, now it's your turn. It's an incredible suggestion, of abysmal proportions: what were Paul's followers supposed to empty themselves of? They weren't gods. They could empty themselves only of what made them human: their souls.

What must Paul have felt, reading back over his words before sharing them? Was he alluding to the *anātman*, paving a path towards India, which was closer in the minds of Paul's contemporaries than it is today? Paul didn't strike out his phrase, and *kenosis* ('emptying', in Greek) became, over the centuries, an important theme in Christian mysticism: an abyss, indeed, to be confronted within oneself – but only mystics gave it sufficient consideration, unlike theologians.

A little under twelve centuries later, Saint Francis of Assisi made memorable use of his performance skills to act out *kenosis* by publicly stripping himself naked: he wanted to show that true happiness, 'perfect joy', the absence of *dukkha*, lies in having nothing, not even an identity (his son-of-a-rich-man's clothes signalled his identity), because we are so much more authentic and immense the closer we are to nothingness. And so Francis brought together *Spells for Going Forth by Day* and the Gospels, Saint Paul and Buddhism. Dante understood this: in his words in praise of Francis, he writes that in Assisi:

> rose upon the world a sun
> As this one does sometimes from out the Ganges;
>
> *Paradiso* XI, 50–51

In other words, thanks to Francis, the Umbrian town of Assisi found itself transported to the banks of the Ganges.

QUESTION: 'Does all of this have to do with being poor in spirit?'

ANSWER: 'The soul and the *ātman* are indeed matters of the spirit.'

ETERNITY

Let's turn now to the *contradictions* inherent in what certain religions say about the soul. The soul, in Christianity, is only partially eternal. Indeed, every branch of the Christian Church states that souls are immortal, never-ending, but that they are created by God; they haven't always existed. They are eternal in a posterior but not anterior sense. This article of faith reifies both the soul (which is created as if it were a thing) and eternity.

> ETERNITY is a word of Latin origin, derived from *æveternum*, which meant 'from another *ævum*', 'from another dimension'. It was a calque of the Greek word *aiōnios*, from *aiōn*, 'other dimension'. By 'other dimension', both Greek and Latin scholars meant another place in time and space, a place that was different, unknown, as yet unfathomable. And it was a beautiful idea, which opened up many new horizons.

Reifying eternity implies taking it as a long stretch of time which, in the case of the soul, begins at a certain point, like a very lengthy subscription. Eternity is actually something entirely different. Strictly speaking, it's a life without time, without a before or after, let alone a now – since 'now' is a dividing line between before and after. So if souls are eternal, we can't say how old they are, nor even when or where they are; and we can't use any grammatical tense to describe them (we can't say they were, or have been, or are, or will be). In this sense, they are like nothingness, given that we can't say when or where nothingness might be.

But Christian doctrine doesn't allow souls to be truly eternal, because this would make them too majestic, too close to the angels and even to God. And yet Saint Paul wrote:

> Do you not know that we will judge the angels?
> All the more reason to allow us to judge the things
> of this life
>
> Corinthians 6:3

And John the Evangelist:

> I said you are gods
>
> John 10:34

Church doctrine would rather no one get too big for their boots. And in order to avoid this outcome, it's willing to turn a blind eye to the incongruousness of a *partial eternity*.

Still, a non-contradictory notion of eternity exists in the minds of all those who are capable of love. It's in their minds not because they have heard people speak about it or because they invented the concept for themselves, but because all of us, as children, realized we were able to love everything infinitely, and we have never truly forgotten it. Loving everything infinitely means that any part of the whole (a family, an apartment block, a city) is too little, and any period (an afternoon, a month, a life) too short for the love we feel.

This love is our immediate, unreasoned way into eternity; it is eternity expressed in feeling. And when we feel this love, we are eternal.

And it's a way of being nothing, because when we are made to understand that we can't always love everything, we begin to become someone – and to look back longingly at that nothingness.

QUESTION: 'Does nothingness love?'

ANSWER: 'No. But the more we love, the more we are nothing.'

QUESTION: 'What about people who feel hatred, or indifference?'

ANSWER: 'The more hateful or indifferent you are, the more you become one of the many limited versions of yourself, as you surely know from personal experience.'

JUSTICE

All today's major religions teach that the soul must suffer some kind of retribution when it returns from earth. The rules of behaviour set by religious authorities on behalf of celestial authorities are so numerous that it's impossible not to break at least one or two, and no violation goes unpunished: divine justice must prevail.

Retribution may take the form of temporary detention (Purgatory) or never-ending, agonizing toil (Hell), or a series of more or less unfortunate reincarnations. But why the soul is the target of such punishments is a mystery.

The soul is not the one to blame: it was the mind which decided to break the rules – and the mind is not the soul, in any of today's religions. If anything, the soul ought to be comforted on its return from earth for the horrible things the mind has subjected it to: mistakes, wickedness, pettiness, lies; rather than face torture, it should be compensated for its trouble. And yet billions of people believe they will one day stand in this invisible dock and fear for their souls – while their mind ultimately gets off scot-free, slipping its handcuffs by disappearing at the moment of death.

Could it be that we all confuse mind and soul? No. Nobody believes that the mind is eternal.

Is it that someone, after all, has to pay for all the evil in the world? If this were the reason, everyone would hold their god responsible, since they were the one who created such a flawed world and did nothing to correct the flaws, even though they were omnipotent. What was the soul supposed to do about it?

No. There must be something else behind it.

When so many people believe in a contradictory idea without seeing the contradictions in it, it's because the idea is a symbol, the shadow of another idea they dare not put into words. In this case, we can see through to that secret idea: the eternal soul is lost when it enters the world of the visible; in the world, *everything* can only degrade it. The soul is, once again, the image of the nothingness that is lost the moment we try to define it.

Then the soul leaves the world and must free itself of what degraded it. Christianity chooses hellfire as its preferred method of purification: the soul is cremated, nullified. Nothingness is restored.

Motivated by anger or religious terrorism, people have come to believe that the fires of Hell burn endlessly, accompanied by a range of other sadistic torments. This belief is equally contradictory, since it makes Hell an outlet for God's eternal remorse at having sent badly formed or badly equipped souls into the world – souls badly formed and equipped by Him. I'll leave this to the faithful to ponder – this is not the place to discuss it.

The more fortunate souls, on the other hand, go to Heaven, after a shorter period of purification. And we don't know what happens in the Christian Heaven, only what doesn't. In Heaven there is no eating, drinking, sleeping, no feeling hot or cold, no working, no lovemaking: it's the most negative place of residence the Western world has ever imagined. Heaven is another reification of nothingness.

QUESTION: 'How can God have remorse?'

ANSWER: 'If you understand it, it isn't God.'

OTHER LIVES

When Plato's *Republic* became a bestseller twenty-four centuries ago, it was proof of just how many Greeks believed in reincarnation. The tenth book of *The Republic* recounts the myth of Er, a soldier killed in battle who comes back to life during his funeral and reports what he saw in the afterlife: the judgement of the dead, the punishments or rewards – each a thousand years long – given for the way they had lived, and the method by which they chose their next life, which might be in human or animal form. Allowed to choose as they pleased, Er relates:

> Their choice was invariably dictated by
> conditioning gained in their former incarnation*
>
> *The Republic* 620 a

Thus Plato brought together elements of a number of different beliefs: the Greek idea of the *psykhē* as temperament and mentality that endure after death; the Egyptian

---

* From *Republic* by Plato, translated by Robin Waterfield, Oxford University Press, 1993.

notion of judgement; and the Eastern belief in successive lives.

The Greeks were fond of importing ideas and mixing them up, reworking them to suit their own purposes. Westerners today don't mind if the idea of reincarnation conflicts with the idea of Heaven and Hell: they believe in both, or at least they would feel they were losing something if (as would be logical) they were forced to choose between them.

And why not? We like imagining angels and demons, and we like thinking the world might still hold some possibility for us after death. We like it, and we don't want to do without it, because we need it to express this immensity of ours, which a single terrestrial life is too narrow to contain.

But why stop at only a handful of lives? Even multiple lives could never match our immensity. Why not all the lives? For our nothingness, this would be possible.

Nothingness is immeasurable. It's not two, and it's not one. It's not in a single place or moment. Although we may find nothingness within us, our nothingness is everywhere and always, in me, you and everyone who has lived, is living and will live: every life is ours. What doesn't make sense about reincarnation, as it's usually conceived, is the making do with a limited number of experiences.

Is this asking too much? Here the old saying holds true: grasp all, lose all. In the sense that the more we realize we can want too much for our nothingness, the more clearly we perceive it.

QUESTION: 'But do people know this?'

ANSWER: 'They don't know they know it. But they can feel it, and for thousands of years have been desperate to say it.'

FEAR OF THE END

Ultimately, there is a need to believe in the soul to keep the fear of death at bay, when by 'death' we mean ceasing to be, and millennial guarantees of an afterlife seem at once to be vain fantasies. It's a doubt that can cross the minds of even the most pious of people, and the prospect of an absolute end provokes horror on multiple levels: emotional, sentimental and logical.

'How can it be that I, who am here, and am the centre of my world, will one day cease to be? How can a world be without its centre? How can a life end so totally and irrevocably? What is is, what is not is not, and the line between the two can never be crossed!' None of these arguments is valid; each is a form of stupidity, in the technical sense of the term; but fear has a logic all of its own, which gives such arguments the semblance of convincing, indisputable facts. What they lead to is a fierce desire to have a soul, even without a religion to define it for you. And sometimes this need is greater than any other: greater even than the need for God.

But if 'soul' is the name our culture gives to our nothingness, then the soul means ceasing to be. And being afraid of ceasing to be means being afraid of the soul.

Out of this arises a situation reminiscent of many others. The strange ways in which we behave while falling in love (being jealous, overbearing and willing to make fools of ourselves) betray a fear of love, which in no way calls for such behaviours. And the anxieties of those who long to be successful betray a fear of success.

We fear love and success because they change everything in our lives: gaining these things marks the beginning of a new phase, and what we were and what we had beforehand suddenly belongs to the distant past. The same thing would happen if someone who was afraid of death-nothingness realized that in order to cease to be, you don't have to die, you only have to look inwards, beyond your 'me': our immense nothingness is always there, waiting to change everything.

Indeed, everything changes if we are also the nothingness. Everything becomes only that which is neither too large nor too small, neither too near nor too far to be perceived by our senses, understood by our mind, described by our words. What remains is nothingness, and it is within us. Because of this, everything might not be enough. And making ourselves believe it is enough means trying to stop ourselves from moving forward; it's the most widespread *stupiditas* of all.

QUESTION: 'So is death nothingness?'

ANSWER: 'Death is only death, and it's part of the everything that is too little.'

EPILOGUE

Analysing Ourselves and Others

TEST

Answering this questionnaire requires no specific preparation, only a willingness to think; that is, to ask yourself questions and wait for the answers. The questions set out here are the same as those used as subtitles to the chapters dedicated to the twelve functions.

It's perhaps worth clarifying what I mean by 'thinking' in this context. When you're taking this test, you need to avoid *reasoning*; I've already discussed the difference between reasoning and thinking on page 37–38. When we reason – that is, when we apply a preconceived logic – we rarely come to realize anything of much interest, especially in relation to ourselves. When we think, on the other hand, we invariably discover new ways of looking at things. And precisely because reasoning means using a set logic which has to be dredged from our memory, it's always more onerous than thinking. In order to think, you need only make the slight effort of doing these two things:

take an interest in the question that's being asked,

feel worthy of the answer which, when you think about it, will always arrive of its own accord.

If you don't feel worthy ('I know I'm not intelligent, so if I've had an idea it's probably not a very good one'), the answer will vanish in the space of a few seconds. It's a symptom of a deficiency in the Internal Direction, Wealth, Authority, Communication, Sense of Obstacles and Overcoming Obstacles functions, as well as in the Outsider function, since the new points of view that thought opens up to us are often considered eccentric.

For each question in the following questionnaire, I give two example answers, one promising, the other banal. The promising responses display a sense of nothingness, of immensity; the banal responses are marked by caution, typical of those with low expectations, who tend to forget what might once have amazed them. Over the years, we all go through such cautious phases at one time or another.

FOR COMMUNICATION:
Do you express what you feel?

GOOD ANSWER: 'Of course not; there's so much to say about my sensations and feelings. Up to now, I've barely scratched the surface.'

BANAL ANSWER: 'My feelings are complicated, so I say what I've heard other people say; it's never done me any harm. When I listen to the news, I don't waste time trying to work out how I feel about it; I just want to know what other people think. If they're moaning about it, so do I. I like the people everyone likes. Late at night when I'm alone and trying to sleep, everything inside my head is silent.'

FOR SELF-DEFENCE:
What exactly are you scared of?

GOOD ANSWER: 'Let me think about that for a minute.'

BANAL ANSWER: 'Oh, I'm not scared of anything, because I've made sure I'm totally safe. I've got a reinforced door, I've taken out insurance, I eat and drink in moderation and when I leave the house, I go back – sometimes two or three times – to check I've turned the gas off. The trick is to steer clear of anything that scares me. Like, I can't tell you when I last fell in love; it's not that love itself scares me, you know, it's more the possibility of being let down . . . it's better not to risk it. The only thing is the thoughts – some of them make no sense, but I just ignore them.'

FOR EXTERNAL DIRECTION:
Are you still able to feel far away from something?

GOOD ANSWER: 'Thankfully, yes. I even find trips to the supermarket interesting, just like I did when I was little.'

BANAL ANSWER: 'Sure, but what's that got to do with anything? New York is a long way away and Beijing even further: the flight's longer and more expensive. But it's worth making the effort to go at least once in your life, mostly so you can tell people you've been. But then, what is there to tell? We've all seen them so many times on TV.'

How many people seem mysterious to you?

GOOD ANSWER: 'None. If something is mysterious, it means it's unknowable. But you can read anybody, not just by their words but the way they move and dress. There's something interesting to discover about everyone, and there's always more to know.'

BANAL ANSWER: 'I don't go digging into anyone else's business, unless they're asking me for money or something. Mysterious! That's a big word. Though from time to time, if I see someone with tattoos from head to foot, I do think to myself, "Imagine going round covered in all that ink. Huh." The "huh" means it's a mystery, doesn't it? So, yes, if you like, some people are mysterious. But not the ones I mix with. My friends are like me: cards on the table, what you see is what you get – wouldn't be my friends otherwise, would they?'

FOR AUTHORITY:
Are you certain of being right about something?

GOOD ANSWER: 'No. I'm not interested in whether people think I'm right, and to claim to be right would feel stupid, as well as meaningless: a month from now I'll have changed my mind about almost everything, because I'll have understood more. If I decided I wanted to be right, I'd have to give myself five or six months to understand better.'

BANAL ANSWER: 'Of course I am! I'm hardly going to settle for being wrong, am I? For example, I'm a Catholic. Why? Because Catholics are right and everyone else is wrong. Have you ever come across a religion that says the other religions are better? We're the ones who are right. And I'm a conservative, for the same reason. I used to veer slightly to the left and that was the correct choice, too; the world has changed since then. It's important to be on the right side in life. The people who are wrong will go to Hell, and who'll be laughing then?'

FOR WEALTH:
Do you want to work or *lavorare*?

GOOD ANSWER: 'I would like to work in an even more fulfilling role, and I'm close to getting there.'

BANAL ANSWER: 'A job is a job, no messing around. I'm always telling my daughter: You have to learn to like your job and give it your best, whatever it is. It's a pact you've made with society; society supports you and you give back to it, rather than going out thieving – though that can be a kind of job, too, in some cases. And another thing: I once saw an old gravestone with the words "Here lies Gaspare such and such, engineer" and the dates, and nothing else. Engineer. That's all there is to it.'

FOR THE PAST:
Are you still holding grudges?

GOOD ANSWER: 'No. It's the same as with ancient cultures: sooner or later they were going to be defeated, but the good things about them remain and are revived when we learn about them. As for personal setbacks, they've never stopped me growing and aiming higher.'

BANAL ANSWER: 'Grudges? Don't get me started. The number of times I've been messed around, treated like a Neanderthal, just because someone was stronger or cleverer than me. Of course I hold grudges, of course I feel bitterness, regret, remorse and rage. But all these feelings have taught me something. The person I hold most against is myself, for lagging behind while everyone else moved forward. History is truly the teacher of life: those left behind deserve nothing but pity. I won't let it happen to me again.'

FOR YOUR PAST:
Do you still talk about yourself differently from how you talk about others?

GOOD ANSWER: 'I sometimes catch myself doing it, but I always realize I'm over-simplifying things, and it makes me feel stupid.'

BANAL ANSWER: 'Of course I talk about myself in a special way. Nobody else ever played with toy cars the way I did, nobody fantasized about Monica Bellucci like me, and so much more besides. I'll tell you my story if you'd like; then I'll let you tell me yours, because I am a kind person.'

FOR THE OUTSIDER:
Do you still feel lacking in energy?

GOOD ANSWER: 'No, if by energy you mean zest for life.'

BANAL ANSWER: 'If I'm low on energy, I take something for it. Doesn't everyone? I know what you're getting at: you want to prove that a drop in energy is a drop in motivation, and there's a reason for every motivational slump. Well, that won't wash with me. A bad mood is no excuse not to do what's expected of me, in or outside the home.'

FOR THE SENSE OF OBSTACLES:
Do you still struggle to set
yourself new goals?

GOOD ANSWER: 'No, I find new ones every day.'

BANAL ANSWER: 'New goals, in this day and age? What else could any of us possibly wish for? We already have it all. Look inside my fridge: does it seem like anything's missing? Cast your eye around the kitchen and bathroom, too. When our grandparents were my age, they couldn't dream of having all this. And what about all the apps on our phones? But maybe you meant new business goals. That's different; it depends on the boss. You didn't mean business goals?'

FOR OVERCOMING OBSTACLES:
Do you have or seek obstacles
which daunt you?

GOOD ANSWER: 'No. The obstacles I have or seek are ones which intrigue me.'

BANAL ANSWER: 'Daunt in what sense? Let me just google that. Daunt: demoralize, dishearten, discourage. Yes, come to think of it, I'm surrounded by daunting obstacles. That is, they would daunt me if I thought about trying to tackle them. But I'm careful not to. I envy people who have and do more than me, and I wouldn't mind seeing them knocked down a peg or two, but knowing my place, as I do, helps me avoid any problems. Still, nice word, "daunt".'

FOR ATTENTION:
Do you notice?

GOOD ANSWER: 'Yes, and it's one of the things I enjoy most.'

BANAL ANSWER: 'I notice if something is worth noticing: if there's a parking suspension, or it's about to rain, or someone's looking at me. Otherwise, what is there to notice? I don't understand the question.'

COMPENSATION

Even if you succeed in ignoring it, an impeded function, or several, is bound to cause some discomfort.

It makes you feel incomplete. You know you're lacking something, but you don't know quite what it is, and after multiple attempts to work it out you come to realize that this thing you sense you need is nowhere to be found. That's because the thing you are missing is not something you can *have*; it's a different way of *existing*.

Existing more fully, as we said on page 70-71, can seem like hard work. Therefore, we often choose instead to adopt a compensation strategy, making use of other people who exist all too amply: public figures, real or imagined, alive or dead. In order to compensate for a weak function of our own, we idolize or loathe a famous person who has evidently developed, or in some way expresses, that same function. For example, loving or hating a dictator acts as an antidepressant or anti-anxiety drug for those who are stupid in the Authority function – a little like pornography helps satisfy other shortcomings. These forms of compensation undoubtedly do more harm than good – those who seek them are resigned to living with their functional stupidity, rather than trying to overcome it – but many of us do it, and it's better than nothing, isn't it?

Over the next few pages, I list some of the popular compensatory figures of the Western world for each function. The aim is to provide prompts for self-analysis by analysing collective behaviours. Given that the figures I mention here are famous people – that is, compensatory figures relied upon by many – one might easily conclude there's no harm in using them in this way: if most of us need this same compensation, that is, share this same stupidity, shouldn't we just consider it a form of normality? That would certainly suit some of us – said famous people and their entourages, most of all. But I believe we owe it to ourselves to pause and reflect on whether using public figures as a form of sedative is a healthy way to behave.

It's interesting to note that now, in our own roaring twenties, *there are no compensatory figures for some functional weaknesses*. In some cases, as we'll see, this is because those particular weaknesses have all but disappeared; in others, it's because these functions have been hollowed out so comprehensively that even compensatory sedatives are no longer enough. In this case, all that's left is a more or less quiet sense of despair – which would melt away in no time if only we resolved to exist.

COMMUNICATION: AFTER JESUS

The image of Jesus addressing huge crowds was long used as a compensatory figure in the Communication function. What he actually said has never mattered all that much to most, as Jesus himself noted:

> Why don't you understand my language?
>
> John 8:43

This question, carried through the millennia, made him a very powerful compensatory idol: a defeated and killed communicator who rose again and ascended to take his seat in Heaven, from where he would look down and judge us all, was bound to appeal to the many billions of people who felt unheard.

But for the past twenty or so years, Jesus's popularity has been in decline; even the Pope doesn't talk much about him. Thanks to the internet, people are communicating more. What exactly we communicate online with the limited vocabulary most of us have at our disposal is a problem yet to be resolved: in all likelihood, most people are communicating the simple fact of being, and of being like everyone else – not especially interesting, but they go on generously and devotedly doing it, regardless. And each of these people can count on a vast audience of fellow experts in this form of self-communication, however minimal it may be. We are, then, living through a particularly intense period, as far as this function is concerned.

SELF-DEFENCE: THE DESTROYERS

When I was a boy, we were surrounded by compensatory figures for the Self-Defence function in Westerns, thrillers and horror movies. We were happy to sit through the silliest of plots as long as they provided characters for us to look up to, who fought off their attackers and emerged victorious. Outside the cinema, tensions were running high: with the Cold War came, for a while, the looming threat of nuclear war, and in Italy the Red Brigades were beginning their campaign of political violence. The Self-Defence function felt fragile.

Later, action films became nothing more than a predictable way to pass the time: the international situation had calmed down and the Self-Defence function grew sluggish. It wasn't that we lacked enemies; in fact, we were all facing common enemies in environmental issues, such as pollution, or cultural ones, such as dumbing down, but most of us didn't see these as problems worth losing sleep over. And there were wars, but Western armies always won.

Over the past few years, the importance of the Self-Defence function has begun to rise once more, with Covid and the wars in Ukraine, Gaza, Lebanon and Iran. Negative compensatory hate figures have quickly come to the fore:

pro-vaxxers or anti-vaxxers – depending which side of the argument you sit on; Putin, and those accused of Palestinian genocide. Yet the positive compensatory figures are nowhere to be seen. They are redundant. Why?

Zelensky, or, if not the president himself, some brave Ukrainian soldier, might be hero-worshipped in the West, *if the majority of Westerners felt compelled to defend something*; that is, if they loved their own government, culture and the life they're currently leading. Brecht wrote in *Life of Galileo*:

Unhappy the land where heroes are needed.

Brecht was an optimist. A land which doesn't create images of heroes but is obsessed by images of enemies is neither happy nor content; it's completely fed up but doesn't know how to say it, or even think it. It only knows how to express this feeling through negative compensatory figures – through destroyers, whom it almost wills into existence.

EXTERNAL DIRECTION: CHRONONAUTS

From the 1950s to the 1970s, astronauts – real life ones, as well as the creations of science fiction – were the major compensatory figures for External Direction. Before them came long-distance aviators, and, earlier still, explorers. These figures fed the imaginations of people who travelled little.

Then, as we discussed on page 29-30, people began to travel more widely and to be less inclined to use their imaginations.

I'll hazard a prediction. The next set of compensatory idols – already waiting like actors in the wings – will be time travellers.

In the 1920s, the eminent psychologist Pierre Janet demonstrated that linear, one-directional time was more convention than certified truth, and expressed his hope that science would soon allow people to travel through the centuries. Rosen and Einstein's theory on the possibility of 'bridges' leading to the past or future dates back to the 1930s; more recently, Stephen Hawking and Kip Thorne (winner of the Nobel Prize for Physics) studied the feasibility of these bridges, now known as wormholes. The stage appears set: we need only strengthen our collective External Direction, only desire a little more – be discontent, that is, in a new way – and the curtain will rise on these new compensatory idols.

INTERNAL DIRECTION: GURUS

The compensatory figure for Internal Direction last century was Freud. With his gloomy expression, big glasses and cigar, his was an iconic image, familiar to all. The theories he devised were contradictory and unproven, but everyone happily overlooked this because there was a desperate need for someone to pretend to examine the interior world, and Freud played this role to perfection: people were willing to believe Freud only because they believed *in* him. Jung competed with him, and for a time Gurdjieff and Rudolf Steiner also shared the limelight. For the little ones, in the 1960s, there was the wizard Merlin in *The Sword in the Stone*.

Nowadays, those lacking in skills of self-examination can turn to any number of compensatory figures, thanks to popular psychology (self-help guides) and so-called spirituality. The demand for compensation is high, and traditional religions are incapable of meeting it. It's a similar situation to that witnessed during the decline of the Roman Empire, when new religions and travelling prophets were springing up everywhere. Now, as then, the thirst for a guru is easily quenched; the only difficulty is in choosing from the array on offer. And now, as then, these gurus' teachings are largely beside the point: with such a proliferation of spiritual teachers, you might expect to see a widespread interest in philosophy or theology, but there's no indication of any such thing. The search for compensation is not a question of intellect but of emotions and feelings. Eighteen centuries ago, between Rome and Nicaea, Christianity was slowly born of such emotional endeavours. Nothing comparable appears to be on the horizon today.

AUTHORITY: A QUITTER

There were too many compensatory idols to count for the Authority function in the twentieth century: every state had its own. In the twenty-first century, there are none: those who hold positions of power, legitimately or otherwise, no sooner raise hopes than dash them. It's obvious to all of us that, generally speaking, the Authority function is in short supply. Perhaps this is also true of our political and religious leaders. As we said on page 42, it's a question of love: we love little, and still less want to be loved. In this case, the person who best grasped and reflected this weakness was Pope Benedict XVI, when he handed in his resignation.

WEALTH: THE MOST WELL COMPENSATED

The Wealth function has always been in a consistent state of crisis among most individuals. Thus, it continues to have myriad compensatory idols, all of them clear to see.

THE PAST: IMMIGRANTS

The only idols who compensate for our poor relationship with The Past today are the immigrants arriving in Europe on small boats. They come from countries cut off from progress, living as some in the West did generations ago. They are a recent and still controversial addition to the rank of idols, scorned by some who would rather see the back of them. All idols have a difficult start before their cult is established. But it's only one short step from racism to idolatry: when aversion realizes its own futility, it may become fascination.

This gives grounds for hope, for the prospect of universal fraternity.

YOUR PAST: THE MISSING ONE

Figures of the past century who provided lively compensation for weaknesses in the Your Past function include Pinocchio, Shirley Temple, Charlie Brown and Linus, and so on and so forth.

Nowadays, cultural demands and what might be defined as 'selective pressures' make childhood seem like an irritating irrelevance. Selective pressures are what we are expected to do, have, say and want in order to avoid exclusion from the group: the most important selective pressure for most of us is having to do, have and want a career, and careers are all about the here and now; childhood is somewhere else, and thus a source of distraction. How many people think of the word 'childish' primarily as an insult they would hate to have applied to themselves? For now, the Your Past function can consider itself marked absent.

THE OUTSIDER: THE CONDEMNED

One hundred years ago, Charlie Chaplin's tramp (also known as Charlot) provided a powerful compensatory idol for the Outsider function. As many will remember, he wasn't so much a literal beggar as the bearer of a point of view at odds with that of other people – including the other vagrants he encountered. Being a point of view many would consider pointless and unhelpful, it might easily have provoked pity and disgust, but instead Chaplin made comedy out of it. His character could have been mere caricature; instead it became a cultural phenomenon. People laughed beyond all expectations, and laughing at the cinema is a means of showing love: millions of people all over the world were worshipping a shabby tramp. In an era of respectability and conformism, the Outsider function was crying out to be fed.

Now, in the most closely controlled period in the history of humanity, the compensatory figures for the Outsider function are ones who make us shudder rather than laugh. They are sacrificial figures, subjected to trial by press – little matter what actual crimes they've committed – and excluded from mainstream society by their guilt. They are foreign bodies, and draw stares because of it. Punished for straying outside the norm, the state assumes the burden of hating them, allowing right-thinking people to stand back and watch with unwavering curiosity. Not that there's anything new about this. Raskolnikov, the protagonist of Dostoyevsky's *Crime and Punishment*, and the French early twentieth-century fictional villain Fantômas were also criminal outsiders. People used to go to see heretics burned at the stake. Jesus reached the height of his popularity when the people yelled, 'Crucify him!'

SENSE OF OBSTACLES AND OVERCOMING OBSTACLES: FAMOUS ATHLETES

The compensatory figures for the Sense of Obstacles and Overcoming Obstacles functions are, of course, sporting heroes.

The fewer goals we set ourselves, the more satisfied we are by watching athletes whose job is to aim ever faster, higher, stronger. The more repetitive our daily lives, the more fascinated we are by the unpredictability of a race. Like other idols, famous athletes allow us to keep living the same old life, existing in a small way. And they are easier to worship than any other idol: they don't require any sense of humour, taste or culture, nor any level of psychological insight from their devotees, only knowledge of the rules of their sport, which are equally simple. As a consequence, everything else seems far too complicated.

Unhappy the land where sporting champions are needed.

ATTENTION: ME

The compensatory figure for the Attention function is our version of 'I' or 'me'. The more we use these pronouns, the more we (involuntarily) signal the flaws in our perception, since it's impossible simultaneously to talk about ourselves and take a genuine interest in who or what is around us, or what's really happening inside us. People who are always saying 'me, me, me' are trying to convey a distinct impression of themselves to others and themselves, invoking that impression and showing it off as it emerges from their memory as from a room: 'Look,' they say, 'it's me, I'm here, indisputably present. I know and cherish myself, dust and polish myself every day, closely guard myself, because nothing is more precious to me, nothing more wholly mine, and I shall have no other "me" besides me.' Those who say 'I' and 'me' believe this impression, familiar to them alone, is what other people actually see, but they're mistaken; the person on the other side of the conversation is just waiting for them to change the subject.

It happens to us all: there is no compensatory figure more ubiquitous than 'me'. And none, therefore, more existentially damaging. Thankfully, it's very easy to shake the habit: you only have to add a question mark. 'Me?', 'Am I me?' and so on. And make more use of the pronoun 'you'.

NOTES

Certain chapters of this book are reworked versions of the first and second parts of my volume entitled *Libro della personalità*, published by Frassinelli in 2009; reworked very substantially, because I understood too little in 2009.

The Anaxagoras passage quoted on page 36 is known as fragment 21aDK.

The passage from the Gospel of Thomas on page 40 is known as logion 2.

The Jung quotations are taken from the last chapter of *Collected Works of C. G. Jung, Volume 6: Psychological Types* by C. G. Jung, edited and translated by Gerhard Adler and R.F.C. Hull, Princeton University Press, 1971 and *Collected Works of C. G. Jung, Volume 7: Two Essays in Analytical Psychology* by C. G. Jung, edited and translated by Gerhard Adler and R.F.C. Hull, Princeton University Press, 1967.

The Kant quotation on page 56 is taken from his essay 'Answering the Question: What is Enlightenment?' published in the magazine *Berlinische Monatsschrift* on 4 December 1784.

The quotation from Saint Augustine, one of my favourites, is taken from Sermo 117, III, 5.

The medieval proof of the existence of God, mentioned on page 125, was devised by Anselm of Canterbury and dates back to 1076.

The quotations from Dante's *Divine Comedy* are in Henry Wadsworth Longfellow's translation (1867).

The quotation from Plato's *Republic* is in Robin Waterfield's translation, © Robin Waterfield 1993, Oxford University Press. Reproduced with permission of Oxford Publishing Limited through PLSclear.

The Brecht quotation on page 176 is from *Brecht Collected Plays: Five (Life of Galileo and Mother Courage and Her Children)* translated by John Willett, edited and introduced by John Willett and Ralph Manheim, published by Methuen Drama, an imprint of Bloomsbury Publishing Plc, London, 1995, © Bertolt-Brecht-Erben/Suhrkamp Verlag 1955, Translation © Bertolt-Brecht-Erben 1980, 1986.

The passages from scripture reproduced in this book are my own translations from the ancient Greek.

<h1 style="text-align:center">INDEX</h1>

ABOUT THE AUTHOR

Igor Sibaldi is an Italian writer, philosopher, philologist and scholar of theology. He is the author of several novels and non-fiction books such as *I Maestri invisibili* (*The Invisible Masters*) and *Il Libro degli Angeli* (*The Book of Angels*). He has translated *War and Peace* and other Russian classics, and translated and commented on the *Gospel of John* from ancient Greek and a large portion of *Genesis* from ancient Hebrew. Since 1997, he has held and spoken at more than a thousand lectures and conferences in Italy, Switzerland and Central America, and he also directs and performs for the theatre. He is of Russian origin.